A
ROOM-TO-ROOM
GUIDE
TO THE
NATIONAL GALLERY

A

ROOM-TO-ROOM

GUIDE

TO THE

NATIONAL GALLERY

by
MICHAEL LEVEY

PUBLISHED BY ORDER
OF THE TRUSTEES
PUBLICATIONS DEPARTMENT
THE NATIONAL GALLERY

1st Edition April 1964
Reprinted November 1964

Printed and made in England by F. Mildner & Sons, London
Colour plates by Partridge Designer Printers, Leeds
Colour blocks by Fine Art Engravers Ltd., London

CONTENTS

Room		Page
I	Italian Gothic	3
II	Italian Gothic	5
III	Florentine Fifteenth Century	7
IV	Central Italian Fifteenth Century	11
V	The Leonardo Cartoon	13
VI	Sixteenth Century Italian outside Venice	15
VII	Venetian Sixteenth Century	19
VIII	Netherlandish Sixteenth Century	23
VIIIA	North Italian Fifteenth Century	25
VIIIB	Bellini	27
VIIIC	Florentine Fifteenth Century	30
VIIID	Early Netherlandish	32
IX	Early German	35
X	Dutch Seventeenth Century	39
XI	Rembrandt	45
XII	Dutch Seventeenth Century	48
XIII	Venetian Eighteenth Century	51
XIIIA	Milanese	55
XIIIB	Venetian Sixteenth Century	57
XIIIC	Crivelli	59
XIV	Rubens and van Dyck	61
XV	Constable and Turner	65
XVI	English Eighteenth Century	69
XVII	Italian Altarpieces	73
XVIIA	Italian Seventeenth Century	75
XVIIB	Italian Seventeenth Century	78
XVIIC	Italian Seventeenth Century	81
XVIID	Italian Sixteenth Century	84
XVIII	Spanish	86
XIX	French Eighteenth Century	90
XX	French Seventeenth Century	92
XXI	French Nineteenth Century	95
XXII	French Nineteenth Century	99
XXIII	French Nineteenth Century	102
Brief Historical Summary		105
Index of Exhibited Artists		107
General Information		120
Plan of Exhibition Floor		Inside Back Cover

LIST OF PLATES

Duccio	The Virgin and Child .. *Before page* 1	
		Facing page
Masolino	SS. John the Baptist and Jerome	1
Piero della Francesca	The Baptism of Christ	16
Bronzino	An Allegory	17
Tintoretto	S. George and the Dragon ..	32
Antonello	Portrait of a Man	33
Baldovinetti	Portrait of a Lady in Yellow ..	48
van der Weyden	The Magdalen Reading	49
Altdorfer	Landscape with a Footbridge ..	56
Rembrandt	Portrait of Margaretha Trip ..	57
de Hoogh	The Courtyard of a House in Delft	72
Rubens	"Le Chapeau de Paille"	73
Claude	Landscape: Hagar and the Angel	88
Velasquez	Philip IV of Spain..	89
Goya	Doña Isabel Cobos de Porcel ..	104
Cézanne	Dans le Parc du Château Noir ..	105
Veronese	The Family of Darius before Alexander (Detail) .. .. Cover	

DUCCIO   THE VIRGIN AND CHILD

ROOM I

MASOLINO   SS. JOHN THE BAPTIST AND JEROME

ROOM III

NOTE

Written at the request of the Trustees, this is the first general room-to-room guide to the National Gallery collection. 1964 is the first year since the war when it has been possible to publish such a guide with the expectation that it would continue to be valid for more than a few months. Minor re-arrangements, however, will probably have to be made, because a new acquisition or the removal of a picture for cleaning sometimes necessitates a modification of the hanging of a Room. It will be appreciated that such things are beyond the author's control.

The Guide includes only those pictures exhibited on the Main Floor. The sequence of the rooms is strictly that of their numerical order. Little comment has been made about the architecture of the Gallery, but it will be noticed that many of the most famous early Italian and Netherlandish pictures hang in the West Wing of the building in reconstructed air conditioned rooms. As a general indication, the majority of pictures dating from before 1600 hang in this wing; pictures from 1600 onwards in the East Wing.

April, 1964   M.L.

Since the first printing of this Guide, the Reserve Collection on the ground floor has been opened to the public. These rooms and also Room IIA on the Main Floor, which is serving as a Reserve Room, are omitted from the Guide. The Guide deals with pictures in all the other Rooms on the Main Floor.

November, 1964   M.L.

The visitor should try to ignore the restricted and for-bidding entrance hall of the Gallery and go up the staircase to the first landing, where stands an illuminated plan of the exhibition floor. Three vestibules hung with pictures lead to the main rooms. Turning left through the West Vestibule, one can pass through Room II, turning left within it, to find:

ROOM I:

ITALIAN GOTHIC

Western painting begins in Italy and this room gives some idea of its earliest years. Before the founder-figure Giotto was born, **Margarito** of Arezzo was working (apparently about 1262) and the large altar frontal or retable of the *Madonna seated with the Child* [564], with flanking scenes from some saints' lives, is signed as made by him. The earliest picture exhibited in the Gallery, it was acquired in 1857, when strong preconceptions about realism in the arts prevailed, as an example—and doubtless as an awful warning—of the 'barbarous state' of painting before the Renaissance. Today, less eager than the Victorians to condemn, we can enjoy the simple pattern-making of the picture and appreciate the decorative effect of, for instance, the spiky brown dragon at the bottom right who is slowly swallowing S. Margaret. Emphasis on pattern in line and colour is typical of all the pictures in this room. All are of religious subjects, chiefly because at the period painting was still largely initiated by the Church. Already there are hints and foretastes of the rising centres of art, each with its own style. The brilliant variety of colours in the late 14th century **Venetian** School *Altarpiece of the Virgin Mary* [4250] already reveals something of later Venetian opulence. The more intellectual art of Florence, with its emphasis upon form and bulk, is represented by the small panel of *Pentecost* [5360], possibly from the studio of **Giotto** (1266 ?-1337), where a complete room, and space therefore, is realised. One can contrast its three-dimensional effect with the personal calligraphy and inspired linear quality of the leading early Sienese painter **Duccio** (active 1278-d.1319), represented by a group of fine pictures. In a glass case by itself is the exquisite small triptych of the *Virgin and Child* [566] where the Child plays with the rhythmic folds of His Mother's veil while she regards him in an ecstasy of tenderness. The three small panels of the *Transfiguration* [1330], *Healing of a Blind Man* [1140] and the *Annunciation* [1139], itself the most beautiful and best preserved, all come from Duccio's Maestà altarpiece, painted for the high altar of Siena cathedral and carried there in triumph from his studio in 1311. There is an almost Persian miniaturistic refinement about the *Annunciation*, with its gold background setting off the salmon-pink and grey arcade which serves to represent the Virgin's house at Nazareth. Reality is not aimed at; symbols do instead, and the painter—nearer Matisse than Masaccio in this—concentrates on lively line and clear intense colouring.

ROOM II:

ITALIAN GOTHIC

Most of the painters in this room, whatever part of Italy they originate in, share Duccio's pre-occupations. The blend of Sienese art with Northern elements produced a Gothic style that became international. Its quintessence is contained in the so-called *Wilton Diptych* [4451], in the centre of the Room, a masterpiece by an unknown painter who was probably French or English. It belonged to Charles I and later was long at Wilton House in the collection of the Earls of Pembroke. The *Diptych* is half book, half picture, made to fold and easily portable. It seems no accident that it is the outside, with the arms of King Richard II and his personal badge of the white hart, that has suffered damage. The interior is still beautifully fresh, and shows the king presented by his patron saints to the Virgin and Child. It is a highly personal object, perhaps painted for Richard II, and must have been expensive. Delicate but strong line combines with blazing colour, and the result is a literal illumination of the whole area; what is not painted is covered with minutely patterned gold. A love of detail elaborates the badges of the white hart which the angels wear—thus seeming to enter royal service—while the king's own badge is carefully differentiated from theirs, fittingly a more splendid version, studded with white stones.

This courtly world, where heaven and earth seem harmoniously one, is shared by altarpieces like the *Three Saints* [581] by the Florentine **Nardo** di Cione (active ca. 1343; died ca. 1365), where S. John the Baptist's brown bare feet make their own pattern on the elaborately patterned Oriental brocade of apricot, blue and gold. But S. John does not quite stand on it, for he has no more solidity than a figure cut out of cardboard, and his feet are no more substantial than the brocade. In Sienese pictures delicately miniaturistic effects linger on well into the next century and there is something still medieval in the seven scenes of the *Life of S. Francis* [4757-63] painted near the middle of the fifteenth century by **Sassetta** (1392(?)-1450). They have a limpid acceptance of legend and an effortless belief in the triumph of saintliness, with breathtaking decorative effect and beauty of colour. No longer is the artist restricted—even in conservative Siena—to plain gold backgrounds. He can paint a sky as atmospherically blue as that over the house where S. Francis lies asleep and dreams of a floating, bannered, battlemented palace [4757]. Fittingly for the life of S. Francis, nature now becomes part of the painter's subject. When S. Francis shakes hands with the wolf at the gate of the hilltown of Gubbio [4762] a perfect arc of birds wheels over the rocky hillside, as if exulting in new freedom. And new curiosity about life in general seems symbolised by the peering heads of the Gubbio citizens looking down from the gate to witness S. Francis' pact with the reformed wolf.

ROOM III:

FLORENTINE FIFTEENTH CENTURY

The break between what had gone before and the new 15th century pioneering art of Florence is seen immediately in the *Madonna and Child enthroned* [3046] by the short-lived **Masaccio** (1401-1427/9) who was, after Giotto, the next great founder figure not only of Italian but of Western painting. This picture is the central panel of an altarpiece painted when he was twenty five. Its revolutionary heroic realism can be paralleled only in the work of his friend the sculptor Donatello, older than Masaccio but working in Florence at the same time. Masaccio's Madonna and Child are a simple sculpted group, as if boldly blocked out from the same piece of stone, absorbed, archaic but unsmiling images. Equally solid and three-dimensional is the throne on which they sit and on which the large monumental Madonna casts a shadow. The Child is at once realistically human and yet gravely divine—taking grapes from his Mother in no charming genre way but as a solemn foretaste —literally—of the Passion. This new realism, dignified, untrivial, intellectual, is reflected at least in the panel of *SS. John the Baptist and Jerome* [5962], which along with its companion of *A Pope and S. Matthias* [5963] is ascribed to **Masolino** (ca. 1383-after 1432 ?) who worked with Masaccio and certainly felt his influence. The two saints in their contrasting clothes of pink and scarlet are positively modelled; light explores and shapes the plane of S. John's shoulder and gives bulk to S. Jerome's hand and the church he holds in it. S. John seems to take the first solid steps on the new 15th century earth, so powerfully is his foot projected, but the earth itself still blossoms with the minute flowers of Gothic refinement.

7

Masaccio's revolution was too stark for the majority of Florentine painters. Even those like Fra Filippo **Lippi** (ca. 1406 ?-1469), who began by imitating him, went on to a much more decorative and charming style, frankly unintellectual, seen in the pair of pictures with rounded tops, the *Seven Saints* [667] and the *Annunciation* [666] which must have been painted for the Medici family. All seven saints seem to be patrons of the Medici, while the Medici crest of three feathers in a diamond ring is on the pedestal supporting the vase of lilies in the *Annunciation*. There is nothing monumental about Lippi's angel, alighted like a pink and silver-tinsel bird of Paradise in the dark enclosed garden before the Virgin's tiled courtyard. Mood and colour are positively gay in a virtually contemporary picture by an unknown Florentine, the *Rape of Helen by Paris* [591], with its icing pink temple and fashionably dressed people who are more *chic* than classical. This picture probably served as decoration of a piece of furniture in a prosperous household and is a reminder of the sophisticated air of daily life in mid-15th century Florence, and a sign of the growing interest in non-religious subjects for painting. In contrast is a public picture destined for a church, the big altarpiece of the *Trinity with Saints* [727, etc.] by **Pesellino** (ca. 1422-1457) which was completed after his death by Filippo Lippi who had probably taught him. This seems to sum up Florentine interests around 1460, with its angels hovering in space, its realised but not emphasised grasp of the three-dimensional, its localised country scene behind the Cross— a glimpse of tree-bordered stream running through a Tuscan valley. Lifting the picture's competence into momentary inspiration is the graceful S. Mammas at the left, his wide-eyed gaze tinged already with Botticellian melancholy. He is probably Lippi's creation, and under Lippi probably trained **Botticelli** himself (ca. 1445-1510) whose *Portrait of a Young Man* [626] is a refinement of the half lyrical S. Mammas. Modelling is exchanged for expression through line. The line sings as it traces the curl

8

of the hair and chisels the features into crisp definition: out of the dark background the face presses forward, sensuous, eager, like that of angels in other pictures by Botticelli. His *Mystic Nativity* [1034] has the same intense eagerness, expressed in terms of almost feverish joy as the angels dance in a heaven of molten gold above the stable where Christ is born. The scene is not sumptuous but simple. The Kings do not wear crowns but wreaths of myrtle or olive—symbolising the peace that has come to the earth with Christ—and the angels hold similar branches. It is like the mood of Milton's *Ode on the Morning of Christ's Nativity* where the figure of Peace appears, softly sliding down to strike 'a universal peace through sea and land'. At the top of the picture a Greek inscription records it as painted in 1500 'in the troubles of Italy' and looks forward to a period of peace when the devil shall be chained.

Although not a Florentine, **Piero** della Francesca (active 1439-died 1492) studied in Florence before retiring to his small native town of Sansepolcro in Umbria. The Gallery is fortunate enough to own three of his very rare pictures, all bought nearly a hundred years ago at a time when he was little known or appreciated. And by themselves, these three would justify his great fame today. The *S. Michael* [769] is only one panel from a large altarpiece painted for Sansepolcro, but standing gravely by itself: sculpted by light which makes each object yield up its texture. The jewelled cuirass is palpably hard—as hard as the laurel crown worn by the archangel is bristly, and as his red felt boots are soft. Piero's eye does not neglect to record the transparent shirt sleeves, clasped with coral buttons, and crinkled in their thinnest folds like shallow water: like the pale ripples which encircle Christ's ankles in the *Baptism* [665], an earlier painting by Piero, probably also for his native town. The gravity of the *S. Michael* here becomes absolute silence. A completely tranquil dimension holds the figures eternally in stillness, and only the thread of bright water falls for ever on to Christ's head. The angels seem to grow from the ground, like the tree beside which they are rooted. Their three heads are like a single piece of sculpture seen from three angles. The *Nativity* [908] is a later picture, damaged and perhaps unfinished, and it remained with the painter's family for many years. The clarity is that of a cold dawn. The Child has no place to lie but on a fold of the Virgin's blue robe on the bare ground; and the wingless angels sing as if to comfort their defenceless naked Saviour, themselves invisible, or unnoticed by the other figures.

ROOM IV:

CENTRAL ITALIAN, FIFTEENTH CENTURY

A later generation of Italian painters, chiefly Florentine and central Italian, is represented in this room, painters who hover between the early and the high Renaissance. They were painters particularly collected and admired by the Victorians who could claim to have rediscovered painters like Botticelli, the Lippi and Signorelli. Filippino **Lippi** (1457 ?-1504), the son of Fra Lippi, gives a melancholy mannered grace to his altarpiece of the *Virgin and Child with SS. Jerome and Dominic* [293], where the landscape is really more interesting than the religious subject. In the background at the left a lion and bear are fighting, and the painter responds keenly to depicting this combat. Nature and wild life are painted more poetically still by **Piero** di Cosimo (*ca.* 1462-after 1515) in the two pictures adjoining. In the *Battle between the Centaurs and the Lapiths* [4890] the tragedy of battle is demonstrated in the foreground entwined pair of the Centauress and her dying lover: isolated from the grotesque battle, half-animal, half-human, they exchange a last and hopeless kiss. With even greater poignancy the idea of lonely death is expressed in the *Mythological Subject* [698] where the faun bends vainly over the wounded woman, as powerless as the mutely watching dog. She dies befriended only by those creatures on a salty seashore where a few birds indifferently stalk; and one is reminded of Piero di Cosimo's own lonely life in Florence, himself neurotic, timid, and doubtless the object of other more robust artists' mockery.

The 'new' subject-matter of classical antiquity became popular with 15th century painters and their patrons. A room of a palace at Siena was frescoed partly by Luca

Signorelli (1441 (?)-1523), and two of these frescoes are the *Triumph of Chastity* [910] and *Coriolanus and his Family* [3929]—each a moral lesson of behaviour. They represent new interest not only in antiquity but in making painting serve as decoration in private houses. From the same room also comes the fresco with *Scenes of the Odyssey* [911] by **Pintoricchio** (active 1481-died 1513) which shows in the foreground Penelope devotedly working away at her loom, awaiting news of her husband Odysseus. The instigator of these frescoes was Pandolfo Petrucci, the ruler of Siena in the early 16th century, and they date from this period. Also by Signorelli is the very large altarpiece of the *Virgin and Child with Saints* [1847], signed and dated 1515— but rather wooden and coarse in handling. All the same, it must have represented a handsome return by the painter to the patron of it who happened to be the Signorelli family doctor. Another large altarpiece, for a Florentine church, is the *Martyrdom of S. Sebastian* [292] ascribed to the brothers Antonio (ca. 1432-1498) and Piero (*ca.* 1441-dead by 1496) del **Pollaiuolo,** whose interests are shown in the almost geologically accurate landscape and the carefully observed anatomical studies of the brutal archers who fire and recharge their bows around the doll-like rather feeble saint. In some ways the scientific studies of Antonio Pollaiuolo, the more distinguished brother, anticipate Leonardo. And, more positively, the Umbrian Pietro **Perugino** (living 1469; died 1523) anticipates the work of his great pupil Raphael. Perugino's altarpiece of the *Madonna and Child with SS. Michael and Raphael* [288] has a calm classical suavity which looks forward to Raphael and back to Piero della Francesca. The cool beautiful blues are like Piero's (see the *Nativity* in Room III), as is the sense of light-filled space, no longer organised intellectually but painted as a golden glow that fuses figures and landscape into a dreamy afternoon mood. It is always siesta time in Perugino's pictures.

ROOM V:

THE LEONARDO CARTOON

This famous cartoon of the *Virgin and Child with S. Anne and S. John the Baptist* [6337], by the great Florentine **Leonardo** da Vinci (1452-1519), was acquired from the Royal Academy in 1962. It belonged to the Academy by 1779 but probably reached England some years earlier. Nothing is known of the exact circumstances in which Leonardo executed the cartoon which must have been intended to be preparatory to a painting. The cartoon is itself not finished, nor is it pricked for transfer in the usual way. It is likely that Leonardo altered his concept of the subject before painting any picture. There is a later painting by him in the Louvre which shows a different composition of the Virgin and Child with S. Anne, and that is probably the final evolution of Leonardo's thinking around the subject. It is not clear what originally were the circumstances surrounding Leonardo's concern with the subject, but some hints seem to connect the concept with France; it would not be impossible that an impetus came from the French king, Louis XII, whose second wife was Anne of Brittany. In 1501 Leonardo was certainly engaged in the king's service, while living in Florence, and a year or two before Louis had conquered the duchy of Milan.

The National Gallery cartoon seems likely to have been begun in Milan in the mid-1490's, and it combines two traditional themes in a combination perhaps invented by Leonardo. The Virgin and Child with the infant S. John the Baptist was a particularly Florentine theme, because S. John was the patron saint of the city: such a subject is shown in Leonardo's painting of the *Madonna of the Rocks* in Room VI. A much older theme in art was that of S. Anne, the mother of the Virgin, with the Virgin and Child. Leonardo here makes the Virgin sit in her mother's lap and yet at the same time he merges their bodies in such a way that their two heads are like twin heads rising from a single trunk. S. Anne's head is almost a mirror image of her daughter's, hardly older and no less mysterious. And on the Virgin's lap—or really, on the two women's lap—lies the Christ Child who solemnly blesses the infant S. John. This moment seems to reveal the Child's divinity, and S. Anne raises one hand solemnly, pointing to heaven as if to bear witness to His divine nature.

ROOM VI:

SIXTEENTH CENTURY ITALIAN

OUTSIDE VENICE

The coming of the sixteenth century saw the rise of great artists in Italy whose names have never lost their tremendous fame. These are the figures treated like princes by the princes and Popes of their period. Raphael, Michelangelo and Leonardo da Vinci are all rightly hung together in this room which might be imagined to be the Florence which was the site of their youthful achievements and which once briefly held them all. Probably the earliest picture in the room, as well as the most famous, is the *Madonna of the Rocks* [1093] by **Leonardo** da Vinci (1452-1519). It comes from a church in Milan for which it was painted—though, like much of Leonardo's work, it remains unfinished—and represents a cool but revolutionary re-thinking of the ordinary theme of the Holy Family. In this strange rocky grotto, where the sun never seems to strike and the plants grow thick but colourless, the Christ Child manifests his Divinity as he blesses the infant S. John, himself taken under the Virgin's protection. And, like a prophecy of the Baptism of Christ by S. John in the Jordan, a river winds away among the pale sugar-loaf peaks. All that earlier painters had striven for in the way of realism is here achieved but transcended—to such an extent that the picture hardly strikes one as 'realistic', so mysterious and personal is its effect. Faces are heightened and refined by Leonardo into pale waxen masks, with glassy eyes under heavy lids; flesh and clothes have suffered a seachange and are tinged with greenish sub-aqueous tones. Even the religious subject-matter seems to have undergone some mutation which makes it curiously disturbing and ambiguous.

15

Also unfinished, but very different in effect, is *The Entombment* [790] by Leonardo's much younger Florentine contemporary, rival rather than friend, **Michelangelo** (1475-1564). Michelangelo naturally thought in sculptural terms, and the *Entombment* is very much a sculptor's painting. The finished portions of the picture gleam like polished marble. The nude in action is really its subject; and the straining figures mould their clothes to their bodies as they heave the heroic corpse of Christ—like some noble defeated athlete—to the tomb. The *Madonna and Child with S. John and Angels* [809], also unfinished, is only ascribed to Michelangelo. If by him it would be an early picture, and it has awkwardnesses like the Christ Child's oddly posed feet. Yet the youthful angels are not unworthy of a youthful geniu3; and there is all the effective simplicity of silhouettes on a Greek vase in the masterly sketched-in pair of angels at the left.

Only rather early pictures represent at the Gallery the synthesising achievements of **Raphael** (1483-1520). The *Ansidei Madonna* [1171] is the most monumentally classic of these, with its absorbed Virgin and Child raised on a high niche-like throne and flanked by the yearningly devout S. John and the gravely studious S. Nicholas—himself the most compact simplified shape. Detail is suppressed and exchanged for more simplified plastic forms, as in the squareish brooch on S. Nicholas's cope which looks as though it had been moulded with the thumb. To break too stiff a grouping, the two saints' crozier and cross slope in towards the throne—S. John's a wonderfully delicate cross of glass—and from the throne itself depends the long chain of coral beads. The same suave authority, expressed with more fluid grace, is apparent in the knee-length *S. Catherine* [168] by Raphael, where the saint's wheel is somehow simplified and dignified out of everyday appearance. S. Catherine has a largeness of design that is heroic and Michelangelesque, but the setting is strongly detailed, even to the dandelion in the bottom left-hand corner. There is

PIERO DELLA FRANCESCA   THE BAPTISM OF CHRIST
ROOM III

BRONZINO

AN ALLEGORY
ROOM VI

none of Leonardo's mysterious twilight but a clear radiance which bathes the figure of S. Catherine as she confidently turns her face upwards.

Leonardo's influence is seen in Andrea del **Sarto** (1486-1530), whose *Madonna and Child with SS. Elizabeth and John* [17] has a quiet and private poetry after the public statements of Raphael. Sarto's *Portrait of a Young Man* [690] is even more mysterious and moody, a harmony of silvery greys which are disturbed only by the veiled yet challenging glance with which the sitter confronts us—as if swinging round in his chair (just visible at the bottom of the picture), a very Hamlet in suspicion and doubt. Something of the same almost romantic air is felt in the *Portrait of a Man in Armour* [895], ascribed to Piero di Cosimo, where the face is mournful and the hand seems to draw only unwillingly the sword from its scabbard. These Florentine pictures are poignant with individuality. It is expressed most intensely by **Pontormo** (1494-1557). His *Joseph in Egypt* [1131] has long been famous and was already praised in the 16th century. Four episodes from the story of Joseph are telescoped within the picture but the story is the least important aspect of the picture. Scarlet and lilac figures animate the emotional architecture—expressed most dramatically by the crescendo of the curving staircase. Everything and everyone seem in motion except for the little boy huddled at the foot of the foreground steps, a portrait of Pontormo's pupil, the young **Bronzino** (1503-1572). Bronzino's masterpiece is the *Allegory with Venus and Cupid* [651] where bodies twine like white snakes against the sapphire-blue draperies, and all the forms have a jewel-like coldness and hardness—renaissance jewels of pearl and enamel, with gold wire for hair. Perhaps the allegory is one of love, but there is some elusive obscenity in the too affectionate group of mother and child surrounded by, but oblivious of, Time and Jealousy and Deceit (the girl who terminates in a tail with a scorpion's sting).

The 16th century in Italy also saw the rise of great

17

artists in new centres of painting. At Parma there worked both **Correggio** (active 1514; d. 1534) and **Parmigianino** (1503-1540) who was influenced by Correggio, as well as by Raphael and Michelangelo. The Gallery's only Parmigianino is the tall altarpiece of the *Madonna and Child with SS. John the Baptist and Jerome* [33], which was painted in Rome when the artist was only about twenty years old. Its elegant intensity is something quite individual, as is its fluid vertical emphasis; S. John's almost dislocated long pointing finger leads up to the slender seated Virgin from whose lap the Child seems gracefully dropping down. The picture's tension comes from these opposing forces. Correggio lacks this effect, and his pictures, like the *Madonna of the Basket* [23], have a rococo insouciance and prettiness. *The Magdalen* [2512] seems to have retired only temporarily from her profession as she beguilingly gazes out at the spectator, sister to the alluring Venus in *Mercury instructing Cupid* [10]. Here Correggio's abilities triumph in frank enjoyment of flesh, beautifully built up like tiny cells of porcelain, but palpably warm. The scene is of some happier Garden of Eden, a Golden Age of nakedness and idleness; and the attempt to teach Cupid to read will fail in this sensuous climate.

ROOM VII:

VENETIAN SIXTEENTH CENTURY

Out of the work of the short-lived **Giorgione** (active 1506; d. 1510) and the long-lived **Titian** (active before 1511; d. 1576) developed High Renaissance painting in Venice. No more than a dozen pictures in the world can be attributed to Giorgione. The new feeling and mood that he brought to Venetian painting is already apparent in the early *Adoration of the Magi* [1160]. While here the Holy Family are in the manner of the older master, Giovanni Bellini, there is fresh fantasy at work in the depiction of the Magi's exotic cavalcade—elegant, personal, jewel-like in colour and costume. A sort of melancholy grace marks the youth negligently lounging by himself. With Giorgione, as with Leonardo, there seems a discovery of the delights of being alone. Even more personal is the *Sunset Landscape with SS. George and Anthony Abbot* [6307] where the subject-matter dwindles to a few colour notes in what is basically a picture of a landscape—one of the first complete ones in European art. Fantasy now heightens the natural world. Painting has quietly emancipated itself from public demands and evokes a private mood of fading daylight in a countryside of high rocks and a mysterious lake, from which some strange creature is emerging. The picture's spell is almost a musical one; its evening sky dies away like fading notes on the horizon. Titian was, from the first, more dynamic, actively working for more than sixty years and dying even then not from old age but plague. His early pictures culminate in the triumphant poetry of the *Bacchus and Ariadne* [35], painted for a room in the castle of Alfonso d'Este at Ferrara. It reached there early in 1523—after Titian had kept the impatient Duke waiting some years.

Venetian art itself triumphs here, symbolised by the leaping Bacchus who springs from his chariot on encountering Ariadne. All the noisy rout as it breaks from the woods, and comes to the seashore, is checked by her solitary figure, one hand upraised. Even under thick yellow varnish, something of the picture's superb colour effects can still be appreciated: marvellous crimson and bronze and blue draperies, and a rich green landscape which drops towards the sea. The drama of the encounter attracts Titian, just as does the dramatic encounter of a very different pair in the *Noli Me Tangere* [270] where it is the woman who advances. The sheer virtuosity of Titian's handling of oil paint makes nearly every picture by him a masterpiece; and it was constantly evolving. The *Portrait of a Man* [1944] is still early Giorgionesque work; paint still rather carefully constructs the quilted balloon of grey-blue sleeve, silken, shimmering, touched with deeper blue in the slashes and shadows. Amid so much bravura the face is a little dim and uninteresting. A much keener perception of physiognomy is revealed in the *Vendramin Family* [4452] of about thirty years later. Paint now effortlessly and rapidly conjures up the textures of velvet, fur and hair and skin in this group portrait of a Venetian family—but of males only. The Vendramin are shown worshipping a reliquary of the True Cross which an ancestor of theirs had miraculously rescued, and they probably wished to encourage heavenly guidance of their affairs. The gamut of age extends from the very old central man in black to the youngest boy holding his pet dog at the right—a child portrait anticipatory of Van Dyck, to whom indeed the present picture once belonged.

Twenty or thirty years later Titian had advanced to a yet more impressionist technique when he painted the small scale *Madonna and Child* [3948]. Here the forms are softened and the edges of everything are blurred atmospherically, while the subject itself takes on the intimacy almost of genre; it is any mother suckling her child in the simplest of settings. Titian's late pictures, like this one, reveal a new tenderness and directness. His quite unintellectual nature probably encouraged his supreme gifts to come to unhindered fruition. In no way was he one of those supposedly typical 'universal men' of the Renaissance. He was a painter, not a poet, nor a sculptor. The subtle autumnal tonality of the *Madonna and Child*, with its bronze and silver-purple colours, reveals how utterly and entirely he was a painter.

While he was still in his prime Venice was offered the art of two other great painters, Tintoretto and Veronese. **Tintoretto** (1518-1594) brings new dynamism to favourite mythological subjects and even to abstruse ones like the *Origin of the Milky Way* [1313], the story of how Jupiter held his son Hercules to Juno's breast and how her spilt milk turned to stars. Though partly Titianesque, the picture is full of new exploitation of the poetry of motion, as Jupiter plummets down and cupids fly busily about, and the milk shoots into stars like fireworks. In the small altarpiece of *S. George and the Dragon* [16], Tintoretto involves the whole cosmos in drama. In the foreground the Princess scrambles to safety; S. George charges the dragon, and the sky above is split open in a divine *aurora borealis* that sets the trees disturbedly tossing. The hero of Tintoretto's picture is light—lightning almost. It no longer falls gently, as in Titian, bathing whole areas in soft radiance; but strikes jagged along the folds of the Princess's dress, spirals away behind her along the coast, hastily pencils in a few gleams on S. George's armour, and finally bursts into elipses of white fire in the sky. Tintoretto sets the ordered spatial three-dimensional world spinning; and the picture communicates a deliberate shock to the spectator.

After his eerie drama, the pictures of Paolo **Veronese** (*ca*. 1528-1588) seem to return us to a calmer, more pageant-like world, but this is not altogether so. The two artists have much in common—not least their urge to break away from Titian's dominance. Since recent cleaning Veronese's *Consecration of S. Nicholas* [26] is seen to be not only a sumptuous piece of decoration but equally a concentrated drama of the moment when S. Nicholas was chosen by God to become bishop of Myra—and a brilliantly-clad angel positively hurtles down with his mitre and crozier. There is something Tintorettesque in the rapid handling of the gold-flecked veil of the consecrating bishop at the extreme right and his marvellous mitre with its jewels that seem to tremble. Veronese's sense of colour effortlessly devises fresh effects in each passage, stoles of pink on white surplices, the deep green of the humble S. Nicholas, and the indescribable range of tones in the clothes of the kneeling boy at the right. The great *Family of Darius before Alexander* [294] is probably the finest non-religious picture by Veronese, and one of the most famous of all his works. It is not an attempt to re-create antiquity but a decorative morality: teaching the lesson of magnanimity which a noble conqueror should show, as Alexander showed it when the family of his defeated enemy, Darius, knelt before him. The classical subject is acted out like a charade by almost recognizable types of the Venetian aristocracy of Veronese's own period. The picture becomes a group portrait comparable to Titian's *Vendramin Family*, but in fancy dress. It is possible that in fact it contains portraits of the Pisani family, for whom the picture was painted. It remained with them until the mid 19th century, and during the 18th century was one of the best known and admired pictures at Venice, much copied by Venetian artists. Despite the picture's huge scale and elaboration, Veronese throws off with bravura sketchiness details like that in the left background of the man on the white horse, and the whole painting preserves spontaneity despite the unanimated frieze of foreground figures. Veronese's decorative ability is seen at its most striking in the four *Allegories* [1318, 1324, 1325, 1326] hung together in the centre of the room. Here the subjects are frankly unimportant and the pictures, probably intended to be hung high, are simply ornamental arrangements of the human body, set in the perspective of unclouded skies, glimpses into an enchanted world of health and confidence.

ROOM VIII:

NETHERLANDISH SIXTEENTH CENTURY

The Northern manifestations of the Renaissance are less familiar than the Italian—even to Northerners. This room shows a number of 16th century Flemish pictures some indebted to Italy and none more deeply than the *Music* [756] and *Rhetoric* [755] by **Joos** van Wassenhove (active 1460-*ca.* 1480/5). These are part of a series probably of the Seven Liberal Arts painted for the Ducal court of Urbino (a reference can be read in the large capital letters along the top of *Rhetoric*). Painted in Italy, they are more typical of the decorations devised there than in Flanders. Another Fleming who visited Italy but returned to his native land was Jan **Gossaert** (active 1503-died *ca.* 1533 ?). Perhaps he had not yet visited Italy when he painted the rather confusedly rich *Adoration of the Kings* [2790] a painting more ambitious than successful. His essentially realistic, almost grotesque style is shown best in the adenoidal *Little Girl* [2211] traditionally identified as Jacqueline de Bourgogne. A less 'advanced' painter, but one with quiet charm, is Gerard **David** (active 1484; d. 1523) whose *Virgin and Child with Saints and a Donor* [1432] has the placidity of having been painted in the artistic backwater of Bruges. It is a meditation rather than the usual 'sacred conversation'. In silence the Child places a ring on S. Catherine's hand, mutely watched by the kneeling donor, Richard de la Chapelle, whose pet dog bears his master's arms on the collar. The only activity is that of an angel— easily overlooked at the extreme left—plucking fruit in the background. Almost domestically calm is David's *Adoration of the Kings* [1079] where the Kings might be only Flemish merchants and where the setting has become patently

Flanders. There is none of Mabuse's elaboration or striving, but a quietly devotional air, the more effective for its simplicity.

While Bruges retreated the rival port of Antwerp flourished, commercially and artistically. Probably it was a 16th century Antwerp painter who executed the *River Landscape* [1298], half real, half fantastic, and perhaps only part of a larger picture. As it is, it makes a pleasing composition; it represents a Northern response to the 'subject' of hills and water and sky. Suitably enough, it shows under the tall tree in the foreground an artist sketching.

NORTH ITALIAN FIFTEENTH CENTURY

During the 15th century in Italy smaller and less important cities than Venice or Florence also produced individual schools of painting and their own great artists. At Padua, where the Florentine sculptor Donatello had worked, the leading painter was Andrea **Mantegna** (*ca.* 1430/1-1506), who later settled at Mantua. One of his last pictures was the long bas-relief-like *Introduction of the Cult of Cybele into Rome* [902] which well shows his sculptural tendencies and his grave attitude to classical antiquity. His figures take on the rigidity of stone or metal. It seems typical that the *Madonna and Child with the Magdalen and S. John the Baptist* [274] should have been painted by Mantegna with a simulated marble framing, most of it no longer visible. As through a window, one was meant to gaze at these statue-like figures whose draperies fall into sharp tubular folds as if of iridescent tinfoil. Mantegna's *Agony in the Garden* [1417] is literally stony, full of forms of petrified rock, each fissure explored and recorded in this harsh garden which in its desolation echoes the agony of Christ confronted by the symbols of his forthcoming passion. The influence of Mantegna is felt in the art produced at nearby Ferrara, typified by Cosimo **Tura** (shortly before 1431-1495) and Francesco **Cossa** (*ca.* 1435-*ca.* 1477). Tura's large, highly-coloured altarpiece of the *Madonna and Child enthroned* [772] was painted for a church at Ferrara, and is almost affected in its elaboration. The Madonna handles the Child with such disdainful elegance that He might slip from her lap while she listens to the music-making angels. In the *Allegorical Figure* [3070] Tura's decorative gifts spring into spiky life. The writhing dolphin-decorated throne is a

25

suitable setting for this fantasticated figure, personification perhaps of one of the Months, and the picture was probably painted for one of the palaces of the Este, the ruling family at Ferrara. Cossa's *S. Vincent Ferrer* [597] is more bulky and less elaborated, but equally lit by fierce light that reveals every detail; fantasy plays its part in the honeycomb of rocks and buildings behind the saint, and light seems imprisoned in the glass beads which hang like drops of water on either side of him.

Antonello da Messina (active 1456; d. 1479) was active at Venice as well as at his native Messina in Sicily, and exercised considerable influence. *The Crucifixion* [1166] probably dates from about 1475 and that year he was in Venice. The picture combines Flemish and Italian elements, and its small area is resonant with the emotional power of both Rogier van der Weyden and Giovanni Bellini. The desolation of the humble mourning Virgin is even more intense as she sits on the ground littered with skulls, looked down on by Christ from such a lonely height. Of about the same date is the *Portrait of a Man* [1141]. Here the sitter's personality asserts itself with no external aids; out of the small picture area it projects forcefully across the centuries, perfectly preserved in the enamelled paint which records each detail of the eyelashes, stubble on the chin, pleating of the shirt at the neck. A private unknown person is given a memorable image of the kind earlier reserved for kings and rulers.

ROOM VIIIB:

BELLINI

The dominating artist of this room is Giovanni **Bellini** (active *ca.* 1459; d. 1516), the brother-in-law of Mantegna, the main teacher of his generation at Venice, and spiritual father of Giorgione and Titian. The pictures in the room give an impressive idea of his achievements, though the Gallery lacks one of his typical large-scale altarpieces. Bellini is also the first in the tradition of long-lived Venetian painters; very old he seemed to Dürer in 1506 and yet still the best painter of them all—and he had then another ten years of activity. The famous portrait of *Doge Leonardo Loredan* [189] is one of the first great Venetian state portraits, at once dignified and revealing. Loredan was elected Doge in 1501 at the age of sixty-five. One of Bellini's tasks in a semi-official post he held was to paint the Doge on election and the picture therefore probably dates from about 1501. Pictures by Antonello da Messina like the *Portrait of a Man* [1141] in Room VIIIA may have influenced Bellini, but his technique is much more subtle. The Doge juts forward impressively to encounter the light which gently moulds his hairless features and shapes the stiff folds of embroidered material over his shoulders. There is a simple but inevitable feeling about the design, compact and powerful as suits a ruler. Encased in formal robes, the Doge is almost a mummified symbol of Venetian pride: a calm, carved figurehead of the ship of state.

Bellini's portraits are rare. His pictures of the Madonna and Child are not only numerous but range in scale from large altarpieces to small panels, and in them all he inexhaustibly propounds variants of the theme. The Madonna may be dressed in red and set praying over the Child who is propped on cushions before her, as in the *Virgin and Child* [2901] from Bellini's studio; or she tenderly supports his head with one hand and hands him a fruit with the other, and a curtain drawn back reveals a castle high on a crag [3913]. At another time the Child sits upright in the Madonna's lap, her knee raised to take the weight, and there is just a hint of a country setting, as in the *Madonna and Child* [280]. Perhaps never more marvellously does the countryside fill the picture than in the *Madonna of the Meadow* [599]; and here the Child now sleeps while his Mother prays over him. The same tranquillity invests the liquid landscape where a herdsman rests, and where a city lifts its tall towers to the sky. Bellini's magic manipulation of oil paint gives a sensuous feel to the crumpled blue and white of the Madonna's clothes, and great atmospheric breadth to the fields and sky behind. The whole picture trembles on the verge of some unuttered emotion: in the sense perhaps of ordinary life going on while the Madonna watches over her Son, and in the premonition that this Child who sleeps peacefully in her lap will one day lie there as a corpse.

In a much earlier picture, the *Agony in the Garden* [726], poignancy is quite explicit. Although still influenced here by Mantegna (whose *Agony in the Garden* [1417] in Room VIIIA offers an eternally fascinating comparison), Bellini makes the whole picture one atmospheric envelope, shadowy, radiant, an almost breathing depiction of dawn coming up in an expanse of Italian countryside—observed with revolutionary response to natural phenomena. We see the inspirer of Giorgione as landscape painter. The first sun begins to seep into the valley, catching the slim finger of tower on the hillside and turning it pink, while the slopes below are still folded in shadow and the distant countryside glows in the greenish early dawn light. In this lonely cold moment between night and day, a single insubstantial cherub floats before the praying Christ with the chalice of his Passion. It is the hour of deepest human weakness; and

28

with the new day comes the sinister line of soldiery, already visible on the further side of the stream. Landscape and religious subject have become fused. In the mystic *Blood of the Redeemer* [1233], the countryside behind the tesselated pavement is no mere perfunctory addition, and the bruised-toned early morning sky seems to echo the subject of the newly-risen Christ who pours out his blood for mankind. The woodland setting in the *Assassination of S. Peter Martyr* [812] is more remarkable and perhaps more truly the 'subject' than the murder of the saint. Although the picture is only doubtfully ascribed to Bellini, it well represents the development at Venice about 1500 of new non-religious interests in painting. Soon, in woods like this, it will be the gods of antiquity who are feasting, and finally ordinary people will be shown having a picnic.

Before Bellini was active, **Pisanello** (living 1395; d.1455 ?) had painted frescoes at Venice but he seems to have been based in Verona. His frescoes at Venice are destroyed and few easel pictures by him survive. The *Vision of S. Eustace*(?) [1436] is probably quite early work and its courtly piety is almost that of the *Wilton Diptych*. In a magic world of beasts and birds the fashionably dressed saint encounters the miraculous stag bearing the Crucifix— all vivid shapes against the dark landscape, and painted with heraldic brightness. The scene is like that from some Arthurian legend, and the same is true of the small panel of the *Virgin and Child with SS. George and Anthony Abbot* [776], signed by Pisanello in the shape of the twisting plants in the foreground. The two saints seem to encounter each other almost irritably, like the owners of two quarrelling pets, and S. George's dragon is indeed snarling at S. Anthony's pig.

ROOM VIIIC:

FLORENTINE FIFTEENTH CENTURY

After Bellini the contrast of Sandro **Botticelli** (ca. 1445-1510), is abrupt. But he was Bellini's contemporary, though he lived and worked in Florence; and both painters shared centuries of neglect before being re-discovered in the 19th century. The specific and strong English interest in Botticelli resulted in the Gallery acquiring at that time several fine pictures by him, including one of his rare mythologies, *Venus and Mars* [915]. It is the quintessence of a moment of Florentine Renaissance fascination with classical subjects, treated here with a linear poetry that needs no pointing out but only silence in which to be appreciated. The god sleeps, oblivious of the playful creatures who amuse themselves with his armour, and the white-robed goddess regards him enigmatically. The picture was perhaps intended to decorate a room, but it transcends the decorative. Botticelli's act of artistic belief in what he has created gives the picture its tremendous conviction. His achievement in 15th century Florence is to paint a pagan subject, with all the intensity previously the prerogative of religious subject-matter. No artist has ever rivalled him in that. His religious pictures are equally personal. With the *Mystic Nativity* in Room III, one may compare the circular *Adoration of the Kings* [1033] in this Room: a much earlier picture, where a whole pageant wheels about the group of Madonna and Child. Many of the faces look like portraits. The horseman seen full face at the far left bears a strong resemblance to Lorenzo de' Medici and the scene seems witnessed, as it were, by Botticelli's contemporaries.

The highly personal art of Botticelli, disdainful of monumental three-dimensional realism, seeking expression instead in lyrical line and colour, had only one great inheritor, in Filippino **Lippi** (1457 ?-1504). He worked with Botticelli, producing sometimes something as graceful as the *Adoration of the Magi* [1124], a wistfully beautiful picture. From his father Fra Lippo Lippi, Filippino inherited his colour sense; here it is delicately subtle and full of original touches, like the kneeling king at the right all in white and blue. While the picture is still in Botticelli's style it is already recognizably by a quite different painter—the artist who later produced the pair of pictures *Moses bringing water out of the rock* [4904] and the *Worship of the Egyptian Bull-God, Apis* [4905]. The latter is perhaps a learned depiction of the Israelites worshipping the Golden Calf, and both pictures are strange, almost wild fantasies with their frieze-like groups of gesticulating figures and their *fin-de-siècle* exaggeration.

The other pictures in the Room contribute more evidence about 15th century Florence, with some further reminders of its fondness for antiquity and allegory. A poem by Petrarch is the source of the *Combat of Love and Chastity* [1196], by an unknown Florentine painter of the period. The protagonists seem not too seriously engaged in combat as they pose like ballet dancers on the flower-speckled grass. More vivid, and more than just charming, is the very small panel of *Apollo and Daphne* [928], usually accepted as an early work by Antonio del **Pollaiuolo** (*ca.* 1432-1498). The scene is set in a very real landscape, that of the Arno valley around Florence, and the god becomes almost a young Florentine as he dashes forward to catch the metamorphosed Daphne—herself a figure still half running, even though growing rooted to the ground. The picture seems to quiver from the sudden impact of the two bodies; and metamorphosis is movingly expressed in the Leonardesque face of the girl, whose hair waves about arms already turned into branches bearing the beautifully precise shape of laurel leaves.

31

ROOM VIIID:

EARLY NETHERLANDISH

The achievements of 15th century painting in Flanders are symbolised by the most famous artist there, Jan van **Eyck** (active 1422; d. 1441) and by his famous picture of the *Marriage of Giovanni(?) Arnolfini and Giovanni Cenami(?)* [186], an Italian couple who lived at Bruges. The picture is signed in legal style lettering on the wall 'Johannes de eyck fuit hic' and dated 1434. The prominent signature is only the first of many clues to the fact that this is more than a portrait of two people in a domestic interior; another hint of solemnity is the single candle burning in the brass chandelier—by daylight. The picture is a double portrait that celebrates an occasion, and places the two people firmly and for ever in their environment: surrounded by the litter of their everyday life—like the shoes and the oranges—and yet lifted out of this by the solemnity of the moment of betrothal. Van Eyck's claim to have been there is proved, as it were, by the scrupulous recording of every detail, even to the minute reflections in the mirror on the wall at the back of the room. The probing quality of his eye, and the marvellous ability of his hand to express what is seen, are found in other pictures by him, equally enamelled too in their application of the paint. The *Man in a Turban* [222], dated exactly 21 October 1433, shows exactly preserved in flawless paint, as in a prism, every crease and fold of the red hat and every lineament of the face. The turban becomes almost a geometrical object in its abstract beauty. The shrewd features have sometimes been thought to be Jan van Eyck's own, and this is at least imaginatively right.

Apparently quite independent of him in Flanders was Robert **Campin** (1378/9-1444), sometimes called the

TINTORETTO S. GEORGE AND THE DRAGON
ROOM VII

ANTONELLO

PORTRAIT OF A MAN
ROOM VIIIA

'Master of Flémalle', whose more forceful, almost uncouth, style is represented by the *Virgin and Child before a Firescreen* [2609] and the pair of portraits of *A Man* [653a] and *A Woman* [653b]. In a comfortably furnished bourgeois interior a quite unidealised Virgin prepares to suckle her Child. The wickerwork firescreen is not only a homely detail but serves as halo for the Virgin—and effects of this almost humorous kind are typical of Campin. Through the window at the left is seen a complete Flemish town, miniature but clear, down to the people in the streets. The painter sets his religious subject firmly within the context of his own period. While the Virgin nurses her Child up in the high room of a house, daily life is shown going on in the town below. The same vigorous vitality is felt in Campin's two portraits, presumably of husband and wife, where it is their personality rather than the painter's technical dexterity that makes us pause.

Rogier van der **Weyden** (*ca.* 1399-1464) was probably a pupil of Campin but worked chiefly at Brussels. None of his pictures is signed but his style is recognizable and was very influential throughout Northern Europe. The *Pietà* [6265] shows the deeply moving quality of his art, with the taut outstretched corpse of Christ caught up by the sorrowing Virgin; and his sympathetic portrait abilities are revealed in the head of the living praying donor who is juxtaposed to the dead Saviour. The two figures are united by S. Jerome's tender hands, one protective, the other helping to support the head of Christ now bare of the Crown of thorns. The fragment of the *Magdalen reading* [654], part of an originally much larger altarpiece, shows Van der Weyden no less technically gifted than Van Eyck, but the mood is nearer Campin's. Until 1955 the background was hidden under brown repaint and the figure appeared alone; cleaning has recovered not only the setting of the room, and portions of the other saints, but also the delicately-observed landscape and water seen through the window.

Two other but very different Flemish pictures command

attention: the '*Donne Triptych*' [6275] by Hans **Memlinc** (active 1465; d. 1494) and the *Adoration of the Kings* [3556] by the much later Pieter **Bruegel** (active 1551; d. 1569). Memlinc's triptych is of special interest as it was commissioned by an Englishman, Sir John Donne, who is shown here with his wife and one of their children. The family were supporters of the Yorkists in the Wars of the Roses; both husband and wife are painted by Memlinc wearing the Yorkist collar of roses and suns. Sir John Donne was more than once in Bruges, where Memlinc lived, and had opportunities therefore to commission the altarpiece directly. It is rare for complete altarpieces of this kind to survive intact, and the actual paint is well preserved too. In a cool scrubbed interior of tiled floor and shuttered windows—rather like Bruges still today—the Donne family kneel to be blessed by the Christ Child, while Sir John's patron saints, the two SS. John, are on the wings.

This quietly pietistic air is positively disturbed by Bruegel's *Adoration* which is, as it were, the noisiest picture in the whole Room. A quite unidealised Holy Family are worshipped by three Magi who are eccentric rather than wealthy or wise. Bruegel's marvellous gift for fantasy makes a memorable figure out of the Negro Magus, with his fringed buff robe as if cut from stiff paper, and out of the present he holds. Part-boat, part-shell, at once a toy and a jewel, this object is like a symbol of the painter's delight in using his imagination. At the same time, he makes the scene vivid by stripping it of courtly associations; the stable at Bethlehem becomes a real stable; the event has attracted a grotesque collection of gaping peasantry and soldiers. Those lances at the left are like an anticipation of the Passion which the Child born into this harsh world has yet to suffer.

ROOM IX:

EARLY GERMAN

Among the Gallery's German pictures, the two big paintings by the younger Hans **Holbein** (1497/8-1543) will probably always take precedence—if only because of their scale. Their association with England almost makes them seem English work, and perhaps it is too easy to think of Holbein as English, though he came from Augsburg and worked in Switzerland before settling in London. Here in 1533 he painted '*The Ambassadors*' [1314], in which are portrayed two Frenchmen who were close friends but who never acted as ambassadors together: at the left Jean de Dinteville, splendidly dressed, fitting representative of France in England, and at the right the more sober figure of the Bishop of Lavaur, Georges de Selve, who came over to London in the spring of 1533. The striking object in the foreground of the picture is a skull painted in perspective. Dinteville also wears a small skull as a cap badge, and it had perhaps been adopted by him as a symbol. The two diplomats are seen here with the whole equipment of a cultivated mind—books, astronomical and musical instruments—and they may stand for the significance of the Renaissance in Northern Europe. *Christina of Denmark, Duchess of Milan* [2475] was also painted in England, but it was at Brussels in 1538 that the Duchess sat to Holbein, at the time Henry VIII hoped, vainly, to marry her. Despite some damage, and repainting of the once clear blue-green background, the picture retains a memorable directness. Christina is posed in mourning for her first husband, and the black clothes emphasise the silhouette effect, while setting off the wonderfully drawn hands—for whose beauty the Duchess was famous.

Holbein represents German art taking its place in a European context. Famous as is Albrecht **Dürer** (1471-1528), his paintings were much less influential than his graphic work, and less successful. The *Portrait of his Father* [1938] is not even certainly by him but provides an image of the rather severe, pious craftsman whose son was to be the first and greatest German Renaissance artist. The picture is probably that given by Dürer's native city of Nuremberg to Charles I—and therefore among the earliest German pictures to come to England. In the 19th century new interest in the 'primitives', and England's link with Germany through the Prince Consort, resulted in several 15th century German pictures entering the Gallery: some as a gift from Queen Victoria. They include the charmingly coloured panel of *SS. Matthew, Catherine and John the Evangelist* [705] by Stephan **Lochner** (active 1442; d. 1451) who worked at Cologne; and, also from Cologne, the attractive *Presentation in the Temple* [706] by the so-called **Master of the Life of the Virgin** (active 2nd half of the 15th century). These pictures are still largely Gothic, dependent on line and colour rather than form. The *Conversion of S. Hubert* [252], from the studio of the Master of the Life of the Virgin, shows a landscape half conventional, half naturalistic, set against a flat gold sky; and yet the kneeling saint's body is solid enough to cast a shadow.

In the sixteenth century, following in the train of Dürer, the German gift for expressive line found outlet in the almost aggressively linear pictures of Hans **Baldung** (1484-1545) and Lucas **Cranach** (1472-1553), both working for princely patrons and both bringing a sophisticated courtly air to German art. Baldung's *Portrait of a Man* [245]—himself probably a courtier—is seen as if under blazing light; every detail of the hair and beard is recorded, carefully curled like silver wire. His love of detail combines with highly original colour in the *Mystic Pietà* [1427], signed and dated 1512. The huge images of the vision set in the tomb and against yellow sky are adored by the lively family of tiny donors who make an interesting frieze along the base of the tomb. In Cranach's work there are hardly any shadows and little attempt to suggest the three-dimensional. His *Portrait of a Woman* [291] is a type rather than a portrait; Cranach makes out of the face a pattern of curving lines that appeals to him. A similar face is given to his Venus in *Cupid complaining to Venus* [6344], based on a Greek moralistic text which tells that after love's sweetness come stings. This is literally illustrated by Cupid having been stung by bees. The picture is only playfully moralistic or classical; Venus is a rather fashionable naked woman standing under an apple tree in a romantic German landscape—beautifully conveyed in the dark crackling forest at the left and the sharp peak reflected in water at the right. The picture's surface is enamel-smooth, almost jewel-like, and crisply linear in the silhouettes of Venus and her son. More intense response to landscape and aerial atmosphere is shown by Albrecht **Altdorfer** (before 1480-1538), not a prolific painter but a revolutionary one. His *Landscape with a Footbridge* [6320] is simply a landscape with no additional subject matter; even more revolutionary therefore than Giorgione's in Room VII. The painter's delight in the wild tangled trees of his native land is subject enough, conveyed with almost romantic intensity. One is brought into direct confrontation with the deserted countryside. Nobody crosses the high footbridge; and only the distant church set among trees suggests the existence of man.

Grouped with Germany are two pictures which are more properly Austrian. Each is highly individual. The *Trinity with Christ Crucified* [3662] is by an unknown painter of the 15th century **Austrian** School and has a delicate response to colour, as well as the soft forms of drapery and faces which became international in Northern Europe about 1410. It is a rare object to find in England; and it has survived with all of its original frame except for the bottom edge. The international-ness of its style is illustrated by the fact that it was at various times attributed to various national schools before being recognized as definitely Austrian. The small *Virgin and Child enthroned* [5786] is in the style of Michael **Pacher** (active 1465(?)-d. 1498), an artist active in the Tyrol, working as sculptor as well as painter. Here the whole picture, despite its small area, might be sculpted out of wood, with its intricate canopies and niches which shelter the subtly-coloured sculpturesque figures. It is a miniature masterpiece, perhaps by Pacher himself.

ROOM X:

DUTCH SEVENTEENTH CENTURY

Dutch 17th century painting is at first glance bewildering in the diversity of its subject matter. Yet it all coheres around the country of Holland itself, not only symbolising it but positively reflecting the people, the landscape, the cities. The political triumph of Holland culminated in the *Treaty of Münster* [896], a crowded scene depicted by Gerard ter **Borch** (1617-1681). Ter Borch shows the solemn swearing of the treaty oath in 1648 between the Dutch and Spanish, when Spain at last recognized the freedom of Holland. There exist written descriptions of this scene which confirm with what accuracy it is all painted here—even to the detail of the Spanish plenipotentiary dressed in grey with silver embroidery.

Proud patriotism is equally but more subtly expressed in the landscapes and seascapes of artists like Jan van **Goyen** (1596-1656) and Jacob van **Ruisdael** (1628/9-1682), the latter the greatest of Dutch landscape painters. Goyen's large *Scene on the Ice outside Dordrecht* [1327] gives us something of the social atmosphere of the period and this is expressed more vividly by Hendrick **Avercamp** (1585-1634), in whose *Scene on Ice* [1479] lively gesticulating people are enjoying winter pleasures, skating and playing golf on the ice. On the other side of the room a whole series of Ruisdael's pictures reveals his range: from the dramatic foaming *Waterfall* [627] to the quietly observed dull day on the *Shore at Egmond-aan-Zee* [1390], with its Sunday atmosphere of people in their best clothes strolling along the beach. Ruisdael's *Bleaching Ground* [44] has an almost oppressive atmosphere, dark and thundery as if from an impending storm, and that melancholy mood of fleeting light that Ruisdael is fond of depicting. People are hardly noticed in the big *Pool surrounded by trees* [854] and the eye has to search to discover two sportsmen amid the rank overgrown foliage. Wood, water and sky make up the picture's subject: a natural world where the only event is the subsidence of a rotted tree trunk into the marshy pool. Always conscious of the changing patterns of light and shade, Ruisdael makes his landscapes more than just delineations of given spots. The *Ruined Castle Gateway* [2562] is almost romantic in the contrast of livid light falling over weathered brickwork, and the dramatic dark shadow that lies across the grass and pond in the foreground. Transient moments of heavy cloud and broken shafts of sunlight are held by Ruisdael in a way never attempted before in painting; and he is an artist concerned almost less with landscape than with the sky.

Seventeenth century Holland was full of painters specialising in particular branches of painting—landscape, portraiture, and still-life—the last a category almost invented by Dutch artists. Jans Jansz. **Treck** (c. 1606-1652?) is certainly not among the most famous still-life painters, but his *Still-life with Pewter Flagon and Ming Bowls* [4562] has its own pleasing individuality of tone, a silvery harmony that is all the more effective for the simple arrangement of the few objects which it bathes. The two Chinese bowls so carefully recorded are late blue and white Ming of a type that had first been imported into Holland shortly before the picture was painted in 1649.

A livelier, perhaps coarser, atmosphere is apparent in the figure subjects and portraits of painters at work in Haarlem, of whom the chief is Frans **Hals** (ca. 1580(?)-1666). The large *Family Group* [2285] by him is perhaps not very successful as a composition and must be looked at more as a series of individual portraits—more sensitively conveyed than Hals' flamboyant bravura brushwork might at first glance suggest. The half-length single portrait *A Man holding gloves* [2528] shows the observation of which he was capable, and it has an unforced impressiveness and dignity. Hals certainly influenced a woman painter at Haarlem, Judith **Leyster** (1609-1660) whose *Boy and Girl with a Cat* [5417] are cheerfully observed, with anticipations of Hogarthian gusto. Judith Leyster married Jan **Molenaer** (*ca.* 1610-1668) and he paints equally gay and now music-making children in a complete interior [5416]. Molenaer was only about nineteen when he painted this picture (dated 1629) which shows him as having already absorbed the boisterous spirit which Hals had brought to Dutch art. The actual technique is, however, smoother than that of Hals' and the paint is handled with great subtlety. Such paintings are depictions, somewhat sentimentalised, of poverty and humble life. Also merry but higher in the social scale are the depictions by Haarlem painters of eating and drinking parties, of which a typical example is the *Party of young men and women* [1074], by Frans Hals' younger brother, Dirck **Hals** (1591-1656).

These pictures are not too serious views of life in 17th century Holland. Real life in the cities there, and the cities themselves, are recorded with utter clarity in paintings by Gerritt **Berckheyde** (1638-1698) and Jan van der **Heyden** (1637-1712), the latter not only a painter of the urban scene but engaged practically in projects to improve street lighting and fire fighting. Berckheyde's *Market Place at Haarlem* [1420] is a record of a scene hardly changed today. Its placid topography seems rather dull beside the glowing atmospheric townscapes of van der Heyden, where light makes poetry out of bricks and mortar. The small view of the *Huis ten Bosch at the Hague* [1914] glitters with points of light, and a soft atmospheric bloom lies over the unpretentious country house, with its formal and yet un-grand gardens. We look over the hedge, which makes an almost witty shape along the foreground, into this picture; and Dutch art is full of such peep-show effects. Actual peep-show boxes were painted and in the centre of the Room one survives [3832], painted by Samuel van **Hoogstraten**

41

(1627-1678). Looking in one can see, across the typical tiled floors of a Dutch interior, various rooms in a house of the period. Hoogstraten's illusionism manages to give a very real sense of intimacy: down to the broom propped against the wall and coats and hats hung up in the hall of the house where a dog sits as if awaiting a visitor. Only a few comparable peep-shows have survived, but something of the same effect is obtained in the blonde interiors of Pieter Saenredam (1597-1665), often of churches—and the *Interior of the Buurkerk, Utrecht* [1896] is a fine example of the almost mathematical beauty they possess. Just as Hoogstraten led the eye through rooms and finally out into the open air, so Saenredam seems to lead into infinity through these high, pale vaulted arches, like notes of music endlessly prolonged.

Landscape, still life, society, townscape: all these depicted, there remained only one other constant aspect of Holland to be painted, and that was the sea which had brought it trade and made it prosperous. Shipping naturally plays an important part in the pictures of Willem van de Velde (1633-1707), son of a sea painter of the same name. Fishing boats are rocking their way to land in Van de Velde's *Shore at Scheveningen* [873] which well conveys their essential frailty between the louring sky and the rough sea. Like other mid-17th century sea painters, Van de Velde was much indebted to the work of Simon de Vlieger (*c.* 1600 ?- 1653) whose *View of an Estuary* [4455] already combines atmospheric awareness with careful observation of the ships themselves; the vessels at the jetty have Dutch vanes, and the man-of-war at anchor at the right of the picture is painted with the arms of the province of Holland on her stern and flies the Dutch flag. Based on the style of de Vlieger are the pictures of Jan van de Cappelle (*c.* 1623/5- 1679) who eventually owned more than a thousand of de Vlieger's drawings. His own technique is highly accomplished and the large-scale *River Scene* [4456] almost literally mirrors the atmosphere of a calm day where clusters of sailing boats float idly on the hardly ruffled water. Van de Velde's *Ships in a Gale* [981] is a violent shift of mood, with its sea boiling and bursting about three ships which have furled their sails as they toss helplessly under the inky black sky. The sea might inspire even a minor artist to paint at least one fine picture, and the *Seapiece* [2587] by the obscure Hendrick **Dubbels** (1621 ?-1676 ?) is such a work. Its sense of pattern is almost Chinese in deftness and economy; a white sky with blue clouds recalls Nankin porcelain, and the glazes of cool colour are set off by the moth-like fawn sails of the few boats.

Across the Room are some of the least obviously Dutch of Dutch pictures, chiefly by artists who had visited and been influenced by Italy. Bartholomeus **Breenbergh** (1599/ 1600(?)-1657) spent some years in Rome, but was back in Holland when he painted the charming *Finding of Moses* [208] with its exotic Italianate Egyptian landscape. A finer painter, Nicolaes **Berchem** (1620-1683), also went to Rome before settling down at home, and he seems to be haunted by Southern effects of warm light and blue skies. The *Peasants by a Ruined Acqueduct* [820] captures, with all the intensity of a vision, a glowing scene in the Roman Campagna. There is an almost rococo grace and vigour about the *Man and Youth ploughing* [1005], which once belonged to the French rococo painter, Boucher. Berchem influenced the landscapes of Karel du **Jardin** (1621/22 ?-1678) who was probably his pupil; the *Woman and boy at a Ford* [827] has much of Berchem's idealised Italian atmosphere.

One of the first Dutch painters to stay in Rome was Hendrick ter **Brugghen** (1588(?)-1629) who was much influenced by Caravaggio (see Room XVIIA). *Jacob reproaching Laban(?)* [4164]—if this is the subject—is an Old Testament scene treated in a consciously genre way, with a new insistence on realistic details—such as the untidy table and the almost uncouthly gesticulating figures. His *Luteplayer* [6347], painted three years earlier, is an outstanding example of a new genre introduced particularly in Utrecht by the Dutch Caravaggists. Its subtle tonality and response to light look forward to the work of Vermeer (Room XII). There is equal realism in the *S. Sebastian* [4503] by another Dutch Caravaggist, Gerrit van **Honthorst** (1590-1656) who may have painted it at Rome. This picture has really less orginality than ter Brugghen's, but is part of the early 17th century 're-thinking' of religious subjects: conceived to make a deliberately emotional assault on the spectator. In Holland there was not much demand for religious pictures, and Honthorst was to turn from them largely to genre and portraiture.

Rooms XI and XII have been remodelled recently, and the pictures therein are now rearranged. While the majority are still in these two Rooms, the following two chapters should now be studied as a single unit referring to both Rooms.

ROOM XI:

REMBRANDT

There is hardly an aspect of Dutch art not touched on by **Rembrandt** (1606-1669) and the full range of his art seems represented at the Gallery since the acquisition of his ambitious, dramatic *Belshazzar's Feast* [6350]. Here on a large scale Rembrandt tackles an Old Testament theme, with a drama of light and shade, and a tense moment of action—not without grotesqueness but with impressive power. And something of the ranging power of Rembrandt's art can be appreciated in looking from the huge Baroque *Equestrian Portrait* [6300] to the small study of *Christ presented to the People* [1400] of some thirty years earlier. One is the triumph of the world, expressed in the complacent features of an officer of some civic guard, who sets his horse to perform a *levade;* the other picture, a study for one of Rembrandt's most popular etchings, is a vivid jostling view of a moment of Christ's agony—conveyed with almost hysteric power. Rembrandt's art was always evolving: from competent and successful portraiture represented by pictures like that of probably *Philips Lucasz.* [850]—painted in 1635—to the *Margaretha Trip* [1675] of about 1661. The glossy assurance of the *Lucasz.* is shared by sitter and artist: a showy surface effect which firmly records the elaborate lace collar and glittering gold chain. The contrast with *Margaretha Trip* is not just between a successful, even brash, naval man and an old woman. The painter's vision has altered his technique. Light is now observed much more subtly and the paint is applied in broken touches—recalling Titian's late

45

pictures. The forms half dissolve in shadow; the sitter's body, her chair, the stone embrasure behind her, only gradually emerge and assemble into recognizable shapes; while the withered, brooding head—severed by the saucer of white ruff—floats out of the penumbra, sternly scrutinising the spectator. Rembrandt even succeeds in suggesting something of the tremulousness of old age with those hands that grasp as if for support at the chair arm and the tasselled white handkerchief—itself serving to break the sombre expanse of robes. The painter seems to share something of the sitter's apprehension of old age, and isolation is suggested in the picture too, despite its being companioned by *Jacob Trip* [1674]. A premonition of his death, which took place in 1661, seems already to hang about his wife.

Rembrandt's own self-portraits mark the gradual evolution of his art. In 1640 he was still happily married and prosperous; and that year he painted the *Self-Portrait* [672] where he stands in rich clothes in a pose probably consciously reflecting Titian's *Man in blue* (in Room VII). That picture, or a copy of it, was in Amsterdam just about the period Rembrandt was painting himself in what is virtually fancy dress. His homely features perhaps hardly carry off the splendour of the costume, and there remains some sense of unease in the portrait. Much more simply did he conceive the *Self Portrait in Old Age* [221] where the actual paint surface is so much more interesting than the smooth texture of the earlier portrait. It was probably painted in the very last years of Rembrandt's life and the features, battered by every emotion, are almost lost in the puffy impasto which drags under the tired eyes. Rembrandt no longer poses or presents himself: he seems to document only the fact of his existence, as he turns to face the light.

Throughout these pictures Rembrandt records the fluctuations of light. In his early work it is often highly dramatic, as in the small *Interior* [3214] where light is the protagonist and there is hardly any other subject. The solitary occupant of the room is reduced to an insignificant blob. Rembrandt himself did not continue with this sort of picture but turned to portray human beings who, as it were, bring their environment with them. The superb portrait of his wife *Saskia van Ulenborch* [4930], probably painted in 1635, the year after their marriage, combines this interest in humanity with new, more subtle, effects of light. The picture seems to be more than a portrait: not only because Saskia is dressed up in green and gold Arcadian fancy costume but because Rembrandt makes a complete composition out of the contrasts of light and shade—witness his treatment of the two hands, one catching the full impact of direct light, the other obscured in shadow under the massed flowers. Saskia emerges from a dark woodland, bringing the light with her, almost a figure of mythology with her sheaf of flowers and leaf-wreathed staff, like a symbol of fecundity—and perhaps it is not too fanciful to think she is depicted pregnant. For us there is a sense of pathos in this portrait of her radiant and triumphant, for she was to die at thirty.

Rembrandt had many pupils, none more gifted than Carel **Fabritius** (1622-1654), himself fated to be killed in an explosion at Delft. *A view in Delft* [3714] reveals his interest in perspective and foreshortening, and this charming little picture may well be part of a peepshow of the kind represented by Hoogstraten's in Room X. This interest in interiors, stimulated by Rembrandt, culminates in the pictures of Vermeer and De Hoogh (in Room XII) and became typical of the Delft School. The **Delft** School *Interior* [2552], which shows a woman in red refusing a glass of wine, is full of painting aimed to convey effects of light—the cleverest being the reflection of the woman's skirt in the shiny tiles. Fabritius's own grasp of reality was bolder, with something of the roughness of real life; it is caught at its best in the *Portrait of a Man in a Fur Cap* [4042] which has a romantic feeling for personality and reverses Rembrandt's usual device by silhouetting the sitter darkly against a pale background.

47

ROOM XII:

DUTCH SEVENTEENTH CENTURY

The large-scale Dutch landscapes which dominate this Room include one of the most famous pictures in the world, *The Avenue, Middelharnis* [830], by Meyndert **Hobbema** (1638-1709), a masterpiece by a painter whose other pictures never reach this rank. It is perhaps almost an accidental masterpiece in its simple effectiveness: a tribute to the way the eye enjoys being led into a picture, as here along the tree-bordered avenue down which strolls a sportsman with his dog. The tall thin trees mark the perspective recession like telegraph poles; and it was lucky for Hobbema that these trees had been planted at Middelharnis some twenty five years before he painted his view. His more usual landscape-style is seen effectively enough in *The Ruins of Brederode Castle* [831], which also shows his indebtedness to his master Jacob van Ruisdael (see the pictures in Room X). A surprising exception to such work is Hobbema's *View of the Herring Packer's Tower, Amsterdam* [6138]—the only proper 'townscape' by him that is known to exist. This, with its cluster of distant masts, captures the atmosphere of a city intersected by water and built on the water; and Hobbema was probably attracted to paint the scene since this was the part of Amsterdam where he himself lived.

The landscapes of Jan **Both** (*ca.* 1618 ?-1652) represent the very opposite of topographical accuracy. Like Berchem, Both visited Italy and his golden *Italian Landscapes* (like nos. 956 and 1917) pay full romantic tribute to a Southern countryside of blue mountain distances and sunny weather. Italy is re-arranged to make the maximum effect of picturesqueness; it remains picturesque even in the more realistic

BALDOVINETTI   PORTRAIT OF A LADY IN YELLOW
ROOM VIIIC

VAN DER WEYDEN   THE MAGDALEN READING
ROOM VIIID

View on the Tiber [958], probably near the Ripa Grande, the old port of Rome. None of these pictures was, apparently, painted in Italy, but they emphasise the spell exercised by Italy all the more powerfully in a flat Northern country. It was left for Aelbert **Cuyp** (1620-1691) to take Both's glowing golden light and let it flood ordinary landscapes of everyday Holland. Cuyp seems to have lived mostly at his native city of Dordrecht which appears in the background of '*The Large Dort*' [961] and again in the more sombre '*Small Dort*' [962]. The light does not quite romanticise placid cows and equally placid peasants but bathes their stubby forms with tones of pale caramel and fawn, until they take on the buoyancy of corks in this airy luminous atmosphere. While Cuyp can achieve this on a big scale—as in the *Hilly River Landscape* [53]—he shows his delicacy best perhaps in smaller details. In this picture the distant group of three horsemen has a positive poetry and mystery. A faint veil of mist simplifies their forms, but their shadows are reflected in the opalescent water; they seem preserved as if between sheets of sheer crystal. Cuyp's small pictures are radiant with skies largely cleared of cloud and reflected in calm water. In *Ubbergen Castle* [824] the ruin is itself almost the only solid shape between lake and sky. The small *Landscape with Cattle* [1289] is much simpler—but more effective, too—than either of the Dordrecht views. Light seems to have washed away the landscape to this slight slope by the water's edge where a few animals and people, equally washed by light, are held as glittering transfigured substances in a tinted prism hard and translucent as glass.

Though the subject matter of the pictures by Vermeer and de Hoogh is very different, perhaps their attitude is not as far as all that from Cuyp's. Certainly they are interested in, almost obsessed by, problems of light. Now much less golden but more pearl-like, light slowly pours into the two interiors by Johannes **Vermeer** (1632-1675): the *Lady standing at a Virginal* [1383] and the *Lady seated at a*

Virginal [2568]. Everything has been refined on by the painter. Reality is very carefully controlled—to a satisfyingly austere point especially in the *Lady standing*. The few notes of cold colour just sound in the bare grey room like single notes of music; and the two women are hardly more than notes of colour—excuses for Vermeer's deft use of his favourite blue. They do not quite animate the interiors, because they too have the same porcelain smoothness of surface as the objects around them; in a sense, both pictures are still lives, and paintings of silence. Vermeer lived and died at Delft. Pieter de **Hoogh** (1629-after 1684 ?) was not a native of Delft but he lived there for some years and produced his best pictures there. Less carefully plotted than Vermeer's, his pictures do not aim at a timeless quality but are more obviously scenes of everyday life. Thus the *Courtyard of a House in Delft* [835] contains a stone tablet above the archway which has survived, though in a different position, at Delft. The daylight is stronger than in Vermeer's muted interiors, and de Hoogh delights in the salmon pink shutters and red and white bricks, as well as in the cool perspective of the passage with the woman gazing into the street. Everything too encourages the illusion that we are present in this courtyard, an impression yet more vividly conveyed in the painting of *A Woman and her Maid in a Courtyard* [794]. This too is probably set in Delft, and the wall at the back of the garden is almost certainly the old town wall there. If the other elements in the picture are taken from Delft, they have probably been rearranged by the painter to produce this wonderful tonal effect, largely restricted in colour to brick reds and white and black.

ROOM XIII:

VENETIAN EIGHTEENTH CENTURY

Venice rightly takes first place among Italian artistic centres in the 18th century and this Room reveals the diversity of talent which it produced, chiefly in the first half of the century. The large views of Venice by Giovanni Antonio **Canaletto** (1697-1768) are partly a tribute to English interest in the city, tourist souvenirs of an age before colour photographs. And English patronage brought him to England where he painted *Eton College* [942] and the fashionable pleasure-dome of the *Rotunda at Ranelagh* [1429]. But Canaletto's *Stone Mason's Yard* [127] is more than just a piece of topography. An early picture in his career, it is painted with enormous response to the tumbled, jumbled Venice which lies behind the impressive facades; and the actual paint here has the gritty quality of stone, while the thundery air of the scene is so much keener than Canaletto's later permanently blue skies. His polished technique is seen on an impressive scale in the *Upper Reaches of the Grand Canal* [163] where the water is like green glass glittering down the long stretch of Canal into a perfectly clear crystal distance in which every detail is apparent. In this brightly-lit way the two feast pictures of a *Regatta on the Grand Canal* [4454] and the *Basin of S. Marco on Ascension Day* [4453] are full of fascinating minute observation; and at the same time they capture the sensation of Venice itself—rising directly from the sea into an immensity of sky. Canaletto's handling is tighter in these two pictures, of which the *Ascension Day* shows the solemn procession of the Doge to board his golden galley, the *bucintoro*, before setting out for the ceremony of the wedding of the sea, then celebrated yearly by the dropping of a ring

51

into the Venetian lagoon. Amid all the detail of the boats and crowds there stands out the slim skiff at the extreme left, with its two black-clad ladies and their standing gesticulating attendant who holds over them a stretched lemon-yellow sunshade. That group alone is tribute to the keenness of Canaletto's eye.

Much more impressionistic observation of Venice is found in the pictures of his contemporary Francesco **Guardi** (1712-1793). Guardi's pair of views of the *Punta della Dogana* [2098] and the *Doge's Palace* [2099] seem all water and sky, with buildings rocking like boats between the two elements. Guardi is more fond of interpreting Venice, offering variations on it and capricious views of it. These shade off into pure caprices, like the three tiny matchbox-size *Views with Ruins* [2521], with their lively figures just points of paint under airy ruined archways. And the same effect is seen on a larger scale in the *Caprice with Ruins on the Seashore* [2522]. The subject-matter of these pictures is much less important than with Canaletto. In the blue-grey atmospheric *View with the Tower of Malghera* [2524] there is virtually no subject: only the frail rigging of two boats and the distant ruined tower break the long horizontal where sea and sky merge. Everything in Guardi seems impermanent and mutable: sea confounded with sky; ruins fragilely falling into water; and mankind runs about no bigger than an ant in this pale elegiac world. Canaletto seems tough and mundane by comparison: his very late pictures like the two *Views of the Piazza S. Marco* [2515-6] are more firmly painted than ever, and they place us firmly in Venice—looking at a scene which is hardly changed today except for different costumes. What is in effect a view of Venetian people often not out of doors but in their own homes is given by the genre pictures of Pietro **Longhi** (1702-85). We see a *Lady receiving a Cavalier* [5841], while two maids discreetly work at an embroidery frame; and the same mildly gallant air is apparent in the *Nobleman kissing a Lady's Hand* [5852]. These pictures suggest a rather vacuous society: people empty of ideas, in rooms empty of furniture. Sometimes Longhi shows topical moments, such as the *Exhibition of a Rhinoceros* [1101], an animal brought to Venice for the Carnival of 1751. During carnival time everyone was masked, and in the *Fortune Teller* [1334] some maskers stop under the arcades of the Doge's Palace to hear their fortunes told.

Venice also remained the home of decorative painting and the tradition of Veronese (Room VII) was carried on there most superbly by Giambattista **Tiepolo** (1696-1770). The four tall thin canvases, which include *Rinaldo looking in the Magic Mirror* [6302-5], must have originally decorated a single room. They are simply meant to please, with their delicate tones and rapid economical handling: idylls of enchantment without much 'story' except for that (told by Tasso) of how Rinaldo became ashamed of the spell cast over him by the wicked Armida. They are full of Tiepolo's own obsessions, with orientals and striped draperies, and feathery trees, conveyed with fluent calligraphic brush-strokes reminiscent of Guardi (who was Tiepolo's brother-in-law). An earlier painting by Tiepolo is the *Vision of S. Clement*(?) [6273], probably the preparatory model for his large altarpiece in the Alte Pinakothek, Munich. Here a kneeling Pope is given a sweeping vision of the Trinity on a great curl of clouds, and earth is suddenly visited by all this rush of brilliant angel forms, culminating in the aloof figures of the Godhead. This particularly 18th century enjoyment of heaven and earth involved together is seen again in the large-scale altarpiece by Tiepolo's contemporary Giovanni Battista **Pittoni** (1687-1767) of the *Nativity with God the Father and the Holy Ghost* [6279], as it were a double Trinity. To emphasise the solemn moment of Christ's birth angels visit the stable, accompanying the majestic God the Father whose swirling draperies animate the upper part of the picture. Equally decorative in animation and colour are the pictures by Giovanni Antonio **Pellegrini** (1675-1741), one of the first of the Venetian rococo artists, who travelled all over Europe. The small but very lively *Sketch for the Marriage of the Elector Palatine* [6328] must have been painted in Germany and is a preparatory model for a big picture in a decorative cycle intended for Schloss Bensberg but now at Schleissheim. Pellegrini painted these canvases in 1713-4 and they are among the earliest purely decorative rococo pictures in a century of great decorative achievements. One can appreciate the rapid zig-zag of Pellegrini's brush strokes which give vitality to the effortless allegorising of a real marriage into this operatic scene.

From Room XIII, where hangs Canaletto's big *Feast Day of S. Roch* [931], one can move into the Vestibule outside and see 18th century Venice confronted by Rome with the *Interior of S. Peter's, Rome* [5362] by Giovanni Paolo **Panini** (c. 1692-1765). The opposition is not quite fair to Panini, partly because this picture is by no means of his best standard. Even so, however, he lacks Canaletto's response to the poetry of bricks and mortar. Painting in Rome was more sober in concept, less free in handling than at Venice; and Pompeo Girolamo **Batoni** (1708-1787) was one of its leading representatives. *Mr. Scott of Banksfee* [6308] is an English tourist painted by Batoni at Rome in 1774. The paint is enamel-smooth and holds the sitter's features like a polished mirror. The allegory of *Time destroying Beauty* [6316], painted in 1746, is warmer-toned but patently sculptural; even the allegory is perhaps harsher than would have been welcome at Venice. But this calmer, more elevated, style of painting eclipsed the rococo well before the 18th century ended.

ROOM XIIIA:

MILANESE

The two music-playing *Angels* [1661-2] are the wings of Leonardo's *Virgin of the Rocks* (in Room VI) and are by one or both of the **Preda** brothers, Evangelista (active 1483; died 1490 or later) and Ambrogio (*ca.* 1455-after 1508). In themselves these two panels testify to Leonardo's powerful influence on painters in Milan; and his influence is strong on the majority of pictures in this Room. The *Portrait of Francesco di Bartolomeo Archinto* (?) [1665] is quite likely to be by Ambrogio Preda and shows in its almost phosphorescent waxen handling clear knowledge of Leonardo. In such pictures the sitters seem to emerge pale as drowned corpses from their shadowy backgrounds, their pallor accentuated by bright, curling, golden hair. Preda's *Profile Portrait of a Lady* [5752] has something of the same melancholy. It is found again in the *Profile Portrait of a Man* [3916], with its severe colour scheme of black and white, by Giovanni Antonio **Boltraffio** (*ca.* 1466/7-1516), Leonardo's principal pupil at Milan. The *Madonna and Child* [728] was perhaps originally part of a large altarpiece by Boltraffio and shows once again Leonardo's influence—especially in the realistic curls of the Child's hair. Traditionally thought to be by Leonardo, the *Christ among the Doctors* [18], is actually by Bernardino **Luini** (active 1512; died 1532), the most popular of the Milanese painters.

Some painters at Milan remained uninfluenced by Leonardo. An earlier Lombard tradition is represented by Vincenzo **Foppa** (active 1456; died 1515/6) whose large altarpiece of the *Adoration of the Kings* [729] is rather old-fashioned for its period, with its emphasis on decorative detail and its raised, gilded, gesso crowns. Ambrogio

Bergognone (active 1481-died 1523(?)) derives from Foppa, and that influence is very apparent in the early *Virgin and Child with two Angels* [1077]. Some of Bergognone's religious pictures are enlivened by charmingly detailed topographical backgrounds—like the remarkable quayside in *Christ Carrying his Cross* [1077B], and the view of the unfinished Certosa di Pavia in the *Virgin and Child* [1410]. Here there is a whole miniature world behind the parapet: a world well known to the painter, who was living in Pavia about the time, and it is captured with special delight in the shapes made by the wandering white-clad Carthusian monks.

One other painter who emerged from the Lombard tradition to produce a small, unexpectedly sophisticated, masterpiece is **Bramantino** (living 1490; died 1530) whose *Adoration of the Kings* [3073] has all the organisation lacking in Foppa's huge picture of the same subject. Detail is subordinated to sculptural effects—even the gifts brought to Christ are large, satisfyingly simple, geometrical shapes. It is possible to see something of Piero della Francesca's style (compare the pictures in Room III) in this rigorous control of reality. And despite the very small picture area, Bramantino's largeness of design makes a big imposing effect.

ALTDORFER

LANDSCAPE WITH A FOOTBRIDGE
ROOM IX

REMBRANDT   PORTRAIT OF MARGARETHA TRIP

ROOM XI

ROOM XIIIB:

VENETIAN SIXTEENTH CENTURY

Apart from the very famous Venetian painters of the 16th century, there were other great artists there who have never so far had the fame they deserve. This Room reveals the achievements of the greatest of these men, Lorenzo **Lotto** (born ca. 1480; still living 1556). Lotto was probably a native of Venice but led a wandering unhappy life in many cities, finally dying as a religious at Loreto. Lotto's response to the personality of his sitters is revealed in the vivid intimate *Family Group* [1047], with its almost candid camera snapshot of the child climbing on the table for cherries. Although sometimes there is a more grave and reserved air about his portraits—like the rather untypical *Protonotary Apostolic Giuliano* [1105]—he is really the creator of eccentric, even pungent, pictures, deliberately 'different' from those of any other painter. The so-called *Lady as Lucretia* [4256] is perhaps more likely to be the portrait of a lady called Lucretia who holds a drawing of the Roman prototype of her name—the blameless Lucretia who stabbed herself after having been raped by Tarquin; and the words on the paper lying on the table are those spoken by Lucretia when she took the dagger. The almost awkward pose of the three-quarter figure is cleverly devised to arrest attention; it gesticulates with urgency at the spectator, as if defying one to pass by. Sensitive to psychological nuances, Lotto was sensitive to physical textures too. In this picture alone Lucretia's dress is a wonderful *tour de force*, while in other pictures the painter makes skilful use not only of the varying textures of silk and fur but also of the patterns of oriental tablecloths.

The atmosphere is much less keen in the pictures by

Palma Vecchio (active 1510; died 1528) whose *Portrait of a Poet* [636] is certainly the portrait of someone being poetical, musing against a laurel-leaf background and dressed in rich clothes. Palma's colour is always richly sensuous, and he—as much as his sitter—appreciates the thin loops of gold necklace falling over the pleated white skirt, and the swollen red silk sleeves of the dress. Palma's people seem always to enjoy perfect health, perhaps because they repose so much and, apparently, think so little. *A Blonde Woman* [3939] may perhaps symbolise Flora, judging from the flowers she rather absently clasps. But she is more woman than goddess: an opulent blonde whose skin and hair are set off by the folds of loosened white shift, itself in turn set off by the clear green drapery that falls about her.

ROOM XIIIC:

CRIVELLI

This Room is given to the art of the Venetian painter Carlo **Crivelli** (active 1457-1493), by whom only religious pictures are known. The Gallery is particularly rich in his pictures which were acquired by purchase or gift during the mid 19th century. At that date rediscovery of the 'primitives' focused particularly on those artists of supreme linear gifts who were to play their part eventually in the creation of the *art nouveau* style. Crivelli's style is immediately recognizable and utterly personal. Its quintessence is in the *Annunciation* [739], a picture personal to the point of eccentricity but with its own highly-wrought beauty. It was painted for the small town of Ascoli where Crivelli settled—and a model of the town is held by the bishop S. Emidius who accompanies S. Gabriel. That the angel should be accompanied in this way is unusual; probably unique is the motif of a ray shown piercing the wall. And not very common, at least, is the concept of the street scene depicted along with the actual Annunciation which seems to have attracted the sharp-eyed child at the top of the left hand steps. Almost like an additional signature by Crivelli is the device of unexpected *trompe l'œil* fruit depicted in the foreground; marrows and apples appear in surprising places in many of his pictures. Crivelli allies to the tight incisive drawing (which records even the details of the objects on the shelf in the Virgin's bedroom) blazing colour and gold. The full effect can be appreciated in the *Virgin and Child with SS. Jerome and Sebastian* [724], an altarpiece which happily survives in its elaborate original frame. The small pictures in the predella below show Crivelli's vivid narrative ability, the minuteness of his observation, and—

in the S. Catherine at the extreme left—the almost satanic grace of which he was capable. His saints are often so hectic and wasted with piety that they border on the terrifying.

In the many panels of the superb '*Demidoff Altarpiece*' [788]—so called after its 19th century Russian owner— Crivelli's art reaches an intense pitch: each saint blazes with brilliant colour, a narrow figure incised and heavily gilded against the patterned gold background. The *S. Michael* is perhaps the most marvellous of all, with his pink and pistachio-green greaves animated by lion masks, and his feathered corselet which encases the body so tightly that it is only by a petulantly restricted gesture that he manages to wield his sword. And he seems sulky with the effort. All these saints were conceived as attending about the fruit-hung throne where sits the Madonna holding her Child who is bent apparently in sleep—an abrupt intimacy in these splendid surroundings.

Crivelli is full of such personal, even disconcerting, notions, and it seems suitable that his *Immaculate Conception* [906] should have good claims to be the earliest dated picture (of 1492) of this subject. This is also one of the last pictures known by Crivelli, and he here sums up all his love of embroidered cloths, fruit and flowers, painted with intense feeling for them, too, as symbols. In such a setting the tall figure of the Virgin seems to burn upwards like a candle flame—the last flicker of an isolated, out of date, art that was to expire with the artist.

ROOM XIV:

RUBENS AND VAN DYCK

The very scale of Flemish 17th century paintings is an abrupt change from Dutch pictures of the same period. One needs space in which to appreciate the large full-length portraits of Rubens and Van Dyck, and their pictures are often reminders not only that Flanders remained Catholic (whereas Holland was predominantly Protestant) but of the close link between Flemish and Italian art. Both Rubens and Van Dyck studied and worked in Italy; Rembrandt never went there. It is easy to contrast his private existence with the public career of his near contemporary Sir Peter Paul **Rubens** (1577-1640), traveller in France and Spain, and England where Charles I knighted him. The large *Peace and War* [46] was given by Rubens to the king, and is a pictorial expression of these aims for which Rubens as diplomat had worked. War is banished and children cluster around the riches and plenty of Peace—Peace herself generously contributing her own milk to the feast. The picture well represents Rubens' inexhaustible capacity to give joyful plastic life to allegory and mythology. There is always a sense of energy running through his pictures. In the *Judgment of Paris* [194] the opulent naked goddesses seem to be closing in on the shepherd Paris, while Strife flames through the sky above, prophesying the Trojan war which will follow from Paris awarding to Venus the golden apple for the most beautiful woman in the world. In fact, in Rubens' picture it is Juno who deserves it, the goddess seen from the back, whose pearl-like flesh is set off by the great sweep of furred cloak, while her angry peacock hisses at the sheep dog.

Energy is expressed more forcefully in the hurtling,

twisting, naked bodies of the *Brazen Serpent* [59]—with its reminiscences of Titian's *Bacchus and Ariadne* in Room VII —where the commanding pose of Moses at the left seems to check the riot of forms. Every actor is involved in Rubens' dynamic scenes of drama: almost ludicrously in the *Rape of the Sabines* [38] where stout contemporary matrons seem rather glad to fall into Roman arms; and impressively in the *Conversion of S. Bavo* [57] where the bishop and Count Bavo encounter each other amid a splendid throng of horsemen, beggars, and noblewomen. All the pride of the world which the future saint is abjuring is set in action around him, and the steep staircase is busy with the press of people. The picture is the sketch or *modello* for a large altarpiece for the church of S. Bavo at Ghent, but owing to the death of Rubens' patron it was not executed on the splendid scale intended. The resulting big picture is tame and feeble, whereas the sketch represents the full vigour of Rubens' imagination.

Another aspect of his vitality is represented in the famous *Chapeau de Paille* [852]—a portrait perhaps of Rubens' sister-in-law—with its intense directness and candid sense of life. Although there is repose in the sitter's gaze and gesture, the picture surface tingles with almost breathing textures of skin, cloth, hair; along the broad brim of the hat the feathers curl like living marine creatures; and the woman looks out from under it with sharp-eyed liveliness, hers perhaps in reality but here conferred on her by Rubens' brush. As well as portraits, and mythological and religious pictures, Rubens painted landscapes and the countryside around his own house, the Château de Steen, which is seen at the left in the panoramic *Autumn: the Château de Steen* [66]. The sky is almost more remarkable than the actual landscape, with its soft lines of flecked cloud and large disk of sun low on the horizon. Autumn might stand for Rubens' own mellow fecundity; and the picture is rich in the sense of evening just beginning to close in after a perfect day. The trees are tipped faintly red and reflected sunlight glitters bright yellow on the castle windows. A cart splashes through the ford—the first of those carts which are to splash homewards in pictures by Gainsborough and Constable. Constable certainly studied the *Château de Steen* in the collection of his friend Sir George Beaumont (who gave the picture at the founding of the Gallery), and its influence is apparent in Constable's *Hay-Wain* (in Room XV). Some of Rubens' own later landscapes are smaller and more intimate scenes. The *Sunset Landscape* [157] shows a few trees reflected in a shadowed stream, and in the dwindling light a solitary shepherd pipes to his flock. This movingly simple, marvellously atmospheric, picture recalls Rubens' last summers in his country house at Steen.

When Rubens died his greatest pupil Sir Anthony van **Dyck** (1599-1641) had only a year to live. He too was knighted by Charles I, small reward for the immortality he has conferred on the king. The huge *Charles I on horseback* [1172] is Van Dyck's most formal and magnificent portrait of him—a dream rather than a straightforward depiction—in which the king rides out with romantic grace, encased in armour and safely raised above ordinary men by his high-spirited bay horse. Van Dyck's own sensitive, nervous fluency gives the vast canvas a flickering rather than swaggering air. And many of his portraits show people a little uneasy, a little evanescent, too refined perhaps to be robust. There is an almost doomed air about the brothers *John and Bernard Stuart*(?) [3605], with their long faces, elegant hands, and crumpled silken clothes. Van Dyck's response to splendid clothes is exemplified in an earlier portrait, painted when he was in Italy, of *Agostino Pallavicino* [loaned to the Gallery], whose scarlet robes almost swamp his individuality. Here the sitter's dignity and official bearing are emphasised. In the *Earl of Denbigh* [5633] there seems rather English aristocratic eccentricity: the pajama-clad Earl—who had been in India—is shown out hunting in an exotic setting. Both artist and sitter seem glad to have escaped from the Stuart court environment into

63

the exoticism of the East, with turbaned servant, palm tree and parrot; and the result is an unexpectedly forceful portrait.

Another side of Flemish art is represented by David **Teniers** (1610-1690) who carried on the tradition of Brueghel in his peasant-populated country scenes, of which the *Conversation* [950] and *Playing at Bowls* [951] are two large-scale examples. These take us into the uncouth reality of a Flemish village of the period, without any prettification or sentimentality. What might seem trivial or displeasing is, however, painted with great delicacy of handling and—at least in *Playing at Bowls*—with keen observation of atmospheric effect. Teniers is a rather neglected artist compared with his popular Dutch contemporaries, but in fact he is superior to many of them.

ROOM XV:

CONSTABLE AND TURNER

This room is restricted to pictures by the two great figures of 19th century English painting: John **Constable** (1776-1837) and Joseph Mallord William **Turner** (1775-1851). To appreciate the full range of their work—and the work of their English contemporaries—one must visit the Tate Gallery, but the essence of them is contained here. Constable was first represented at the National Gallery in the year of his death when *The Cornfield* [130] was presented in his memory. It had been exhibited at the Royal Academy in 1826 and stands for the most 'finished' type of Constable landscape; a view of his native Suffolk recorded with passionate feeling for tangled hedgerows, fields of heavy corn, the shifting summer sky. Because of Constable's seriousness of purpose it is, in his own words, 'not neglected in any part'. The detail gives the picture almost moral conviction, as well as providing a view of rich pastoral England untouched by the Industrial Revolution. Indeed, the two go together in Constable who is always building, as it were, a fresher, and better, country world where life is peaceful. There is a sense of peaceful permanence in the large-scale *Hay-Wain* [1207] which is a scene that the painter grew up with; it shows the mill stream at East Bergholt just by Flatford Mill where Constable was born. At the left is Willy Lott's house, itself almost a symbol of permanence, for Willy Lott was born long before Constable, lived all his life in this house and died finally, aged 88, after Constable's own death. As well as being an elaborate statement of Constable's own convictions, the *Hay-Wain* represents on a grand scale the 19th century rediscovery of landscape as a worthy subject for art. The picture was exhibited at the Salon in Paris in 1824 and created considerable stir among critics and painters. Constable was awarded a gold medal for it; a cast of this medal was inset in the frame.

The less public side of Constable's art is represented by sketches like that of *Salisbury Cathedral* [2651]. This too has a personal association, for the painter's great friend Archdeacon Fisher lived in the house seen here through the trees, and it is his lawn that extends down to the river's edge. The picture was painted on the spot in the summer of 1820. Detail is suppressed in exchange for rapid grasp of form and capture of the moment: sunlight striking the cathedral tower, a slight breeze ruffling the heavy-foliaged trees, and clouds drifting in a bright sky. It is a picture to make one appreciate Henry James's remark that the two most beautiful words in the English language are 'summer afternoon'. Constable's fascination with the ever-changing pattern of clouds is shown vividly in *Weymouth Bay* [2652], a picture painted in 1816 when he spent his honeymoon near Weymouth. Here the coast is a mere strip of summarily indicated foreground, and it is the smoky spiral of clouds that suggests a deep aerial perspective. Out of these simple elements Constable makes his picture. The weather becomes a subject in itself. A brilliant summer day in the country is sufficient in *Stoke-by-Nayland* [2649]—which gives an almost physical sensation of hot sunlight. A sudden bar of shadow falling over the sea is sufficient in the small *View of Harwich* [1276], where the ramshackle low lighthouse building stands frailly between the elements of air and water.

Constable never travelled outside England. He was slow to develop as an artist, and slow to become famous. In all these things he was the very opposite of Turner. If he was Wordsworthian in his attitude to nature, Turner was Byronic. The elements which seem so domesticated in Constable's pictures are at their most extreme and battling in Turner's grandest pictures. The large *Fire at Sea* [558] depicts man's hopeless fight amid storm and disaster.

Human beings are literal flotsam in a raging sea. Turner himself actually experienced the *Snow Storm at Sea* [530] in which wind and snow and spray sport with the unfortunate steam-boat until it is barely visible except for a straining mast. There is a tremendous exhilarating terror in this moment when all nature's forces are unleashed. Something of the same drama is in *Rain, Steam and Speed* [538], where the glowing train forces its way over the high viaduct through the driving mist and rain—and here man is winning through, thanks to the newly invented steam engine. But Turner's intense receptivity to nature's moods made him able to capture also moments of utter tranquillity. In the *Evening Star* [1991] there is nothing but the merging of sea and sky, day and night, as evening slowly sucks the colour from things; and only the diamond point of the single star shines out, caught tremblingly on the dark water. The same poignancy hovers about *The 'Fighting Téméraire'* [524] in which between dusk and day an old ship is tugged to its last berth. The ghostly hulk floats over the calm glassy sea, and the sun sinks like a bonfire in the west, seeming a symbol of the life that is ended, stirring us to a quite irrational sadness for days gone by. Such is Turner's **poetry**.

In the large-scale *Ulysses deriding Polyphemus* [508], Turner takes a classical subject but turns it into a great Wagnerian theatre of the elements where Ulysses' ship is dwarfed by the prismatic cavern of the sunset sky, and led out of danger over the glistening water by the clustering, phosphorescent sea nymphs. Up at the left rages the giant Polyphemus, whom Ulysses had blinded, a shadowy elemental figure compounded out of cloud shapes and rock. The picture is all fire and light and cloud. Turner is always for banishing the solid earth Constable loved to depict. Even the ostensibly ordinary English scene of *Sunset at Petworth* [2701]—painted in the grounds of the house of Turner's patron Lord Egremont—becomes a magic moment of departing day. At the centre the hot white circle of the sun seems to be flooding with autumnal colour the atmospheric envelope of sky and the pale lake, fringed by a few tufts of tree. The atmosphere is all the time dissolving while we watch. Constable asserts an almost oak-like, deep-rooted love of the permanent and the peaceful, but Turner exults in a world where nothing stands still.

ROOM XVI:

ENGLISH EIGHTEENTH CENTURY

Many of the pictures in this Room first appeared in the exhibitions at the Royal Academy (founded in 1768). Inevitably, the majority are portraits because this was the standard requirement of English 18th century patrons, supplemented by some requests for the portrayal of their domestic animals and their houses. The first President of the Royal Academy was Sir Joshua **Reynolds** (1723-1792), almost entirely a painter of portraits but of portraits that try to give the sitter a definite role and present him or her to the public as a personality. The full length of *Captain Robert Orme* [681] was painted in 1756 when Captain Orme was rather a hero—having returned to England from America where he had gallantly rescued General Braddock's body during an encounter in the war with the French. Sitter and painter were both young, and Reynolds responds—as always—to painting a young man. Captain Orme is more pensive than heroic; his face is painted with great delicacy, and the picture's quiet air may be contrasted with the bravura of another much later military portrait by Reynolds, *General Sir Banastre Tarleton* [5985], painted in 1782. Tarleton had figured in the American War of Independence and Reynolds shows him in the uniform of a troop known as Tarleton's Green Horse. Reynolds shows him also in the midst of battle, with frightened horses, cannon, the swirl of smoke and flags, an interesting 'engaged' concept which looks forward to 19th century romantic painting.

Between these two portraits the very large *Three Ladies adorning a Term of Hymen* [79] is a bit of a bore, an uneasy mixture of portrait and allegory. The ladies are the Montgomery sisters, who were brought up in Ireland and known as 'The Irish Graces'. Even they do not seem quite at ease in the task of wreathing a term of Hymen which rather perversely is set beyond their reach; and perhaps Reynolds felt some embarrassment about the commission he had been given by the fiancé of the eldest sister. For all his ambitious ideas, Reynolds was happier presenting the straightforward group of *Sir Watkin Williams-Wynn and his Mother* [5750] with its unusual landscape background which is probably intended to suggest the Welsh country-side near the Williams-Wynn house. Reynolds' half length portraits are more succinct statements about the people depicted, and their sheer range is revealed by comparing the family group of *Lady Cockburn and her Children* [2077], with the intimate directness and unposed quality of *Anne, Countess of Albemarle* [1259], and this portrait in turn with the bluff and sturdy *Lord Heathfield* [111]. Lady Cockburn nurses her children with a rather conscious air, and even the children seem acting a spontaneity that is unfelt. The design of the picture is contrived, whereas that of Lady Albemarle is utterly simple: a plainly-dressed middle-aged lady is shown doing some knitting, and the picture gains from the unforced dignity of the plain setting, the commonplace occupation. If Lady Albemarle is retiring and domestic, Lord Heathfield is out on the public stage; but he holds his place there confidently. The picture was painted in 1787, the year he received a peerage. He had already been Governor of Gibraltar, sustaining a famous siege there a few years earlier. He clasps the key to the fortress he had not surrendered, while the background billows with cannon smoke. In each of these three very different portraits Reynolds finds a fresh solution to painting the face. He always had difficulty in getting good likenesses and perhaps this positively encouraged him to make something more than a mere likeness out of his portraits.

His great contemporary Thomas **Gainsborough** (1727-1788) never had any difficulty with a likeness, nor did he restrict his work to portraiture. By the time he had finished with his English sitters they actually looked elegant. To the prosaic fact of Reynolds' *Sir Watkin and his Mother*, Gainsborough might be said to oppose the enchantment of *The Morning Walk* [6209], in which young Mr. Hallett and his bride, accompanied by an elegant silk-furred dog, walk in a woodland of silk and feathers hardly more solid than the plumes and ribbon in Mrs. Hallett's hat. This picture was painted in London in 1785/6, just after the couple's marriage, and represents the quintessence of Gainsborough's late feathery style, all gleams and suggestions: painting in which the brushwork seems to ripple over the surface of the canvas. The picture marks the distance Gainsborough had come in handling since the days of his early masterpiece of another couple *Mr. and Mrs. Andrews* [6301], painted about 1750 and in Suffolk. In that Gainsborough depicts the sitters with almost naive intensity: setting them down solidly on their feet in the autumnal countryside, juxtaposed to the freshly reaped cornfield which is shown with the same enchanting literalness as are the figures of the squire and his wife. The picture is a masterpiece and a portrait not only of people but of land. In the same way, sitter and countryside are blended in *Mr. Plampin* [5984], another early Suffolk picture. Gainsborough seems anxious to get his sitters out of the studio and into daylight. He preserves their rustic environment; and part of the charm of these portraits is the way in which nothing is softened or flattered; they have a candour that is at once amusing and touching. Gainsborough's 'Dutch' style of landscape in *Cornard Wood* [925], a picture said to have been begun when he was only thirteen, has this directness. By the time of the *The Watering Place* [109], exhibited at the Royal Academy in 1777, the forms have become more elegant and evanescent. Almost ghostly cows come to drink at a pool not so much of water as of watered-silk. Gainsborough's style of painting was always evolving; and he moved far away from the detailed solid manner of his early work. He retained a lively interest in people and character which is typical of his century. He was naturally drawn to children and animals—and the *White Dogs* [5844] is made vivid by affection as well as by beautiful painting. In his portraits of his two daughters Mary and Margaret there is a haunting tenderness which suggests awareness already of their eccentricity. *The Painter's Daughter, Mary* [5638] shows the elder girl grown up, a year or two before she married, unhappily, the musician Fischer. The two young girls seem to protect each other as they cradle a cat in the small, unfinished bust-length [3812], staring out rather moodily. The larger *Painter's Daughters chasing a butterfly* [1811] is also unfinished—yet lack of finish is part of its ravishing spontaneity and speed. Like the children, paint runs in its rapid evocation of a wood, the silvery-lemon dresses, and the solemn, un-pretty faces. The result is a masterpiece of a completely absorbed childhood moment.

A whole society is depicted in the work of William **Hogarth** (1697-1764), seen satirically but judged morally. His famous series of six pictures *Marriage à la Mode* [113-8], is really a novel in paint, telling the story of the marriage of an Earl's son and a city merchant's daughter, a marriage made for reasons of vanity and money. Hogarth indicts high life with real feeling and moral fervour; the last two pictures show the murder of the Earl, stabbed by his wife's lover, and the suicide of his wife after her lover has been hanged. Despite the satirical, often amusing, details, the painter's purpose is serious. He expects his pictures to be read; and they are perhaps over-full of allusions. At the same time, Hogarth remained an artist, and passages of painting—especially in *Shortly after the Marriage* [114] and the *Countess's Morning Levée* [116]—show how attractively he could paint. The free handling of the *Shrimp Girl* [1162] is combined with cockney vivacity: the girl is brushed onto the canvas in a vigorous Impressionistic style.

DE HOOGH   COURTYARD OF A HOUSE IN DELFT

ROOM XII

RUBENS   "LE CHAPEAU DE PAILLE"

ROOM XIV

ROOM XVII (the Dome):

ITALIAN ALTARPIECES

In the centre stands a French bronze statue of *Fame* [4105], possibly by Guillaume **Bertelot** (d. 1648). Four important large 16th century Italian altarpieces are hung on the surrounding walls, somewhat suffering aesthetically from being out of their church environment. It is not known what church originally contained the *Madonna and Child with S. Bernardino and other Saints* [625] by **Moretto** (c. 1498-1554), a leading painter of Brescia. His saints are strongly individualised—not surprisingly in an artist who was a distinguished portrait-painter—and painted with great plastic force. Earth perhaps was more sympathetic to Moretto than ideas of heaven; and he makes a formally beautiful still-life out of the three mitres at S. Bernardino's feet—symbolising the three bishoprics the saint rejected. The altarpiece of the *Virgin and Child with S. Anne and other Saints* [179], with a lunette above, the *Pietà* [180], comes from a church at Lucca but was painted by the Bolognese Francesco **Francia** (*ca.* 1450-1517/8) late in his career. It is softer and more yielding than Moretto's picture. The group of Madonna, Child and S. Anne are, as it were, a remodelling of the group in Leonardo's famous cartoon (in Room V): but worked in wax, and without Leonardo's magic aura. It was for the church of S. William at Ferrara that the *Madonna and Child with S. William and other Saints* [671] was painted by the Ferrarese artist **Garofalo** (1481(?)-1559). S. William was a Duke of Aquitaine who fought against the Moors and then became a monk; he is the rather shy youthful figure in armour at the extreme left of the picture. He seems to appear again in the large altarpiece of the *Madonna and Child enthroned* [119] by

Lorenzo **Costa** (1459/60-1535), where the saint in armour has been identified as him. This picture also comes from Ferrara, and it is a much grander and more elaborate work than Garofalo's. It is quite likely that parts of the picture—notably the reliefs round the throne—are by another painter, Gian Francesco de' **Maineri** (recorded 1489 to 1506) who may well have begun the whole work. The result is not totally satisfactory, but the culmination of the composition is impressive: with the noble standing Christ Child solemnly blessing the world.

ROOM XVIIA:

ITALIAN SEVENTEENTH CENTURY

The centrally placed *Supper at Emmaus* [172] by **Caravaggio** (1573-1610) immediately draws the spectator's attention by its *trompe l'œil* realism. It brings one to stand at the table, as if present at the explosive moment in the inn at Emmaus when Christ blessed the food and revealed his divinity. By itself the picture sums up Caravaggio's revolutionary style of painting which makes him a pioneer of realism in 17th century Europe. The Disciples are depicted as simple poor men—the torn sleeve of the left-hand apostle sharply catches the light. And the still life is vividly detailed on the expanse of white tablecloth. The drama of the gesturing group tightly packed about the table is emphasised by the strong contrasts of light which throw dark shadows on the wall and set off the central full face of Christ. The picture is an early one by an artist who died prematurely. Much later work, probably from his last year or so, is the restrained *Salome with the Head of S. John the Baptist* [loaned to the Gallery] where colour is now much less bright, and the light has lost its hard glittering quality. The drama is of muted poignancy, and all the actors seem saddened by what has occurred. Both pictures treat the familiar subject-matter of New Testament scenes with powerful originality: in conception, in execution, and in mood. Caravaggio's art could not fail to excite. It created tremendous effect at Rome in the early years of the 17th century, on foreign artists as well as native Italians. There is an echo of it in Le **Valentin** (1591(?)-1632), whose *Four Ages of Man* [4919] has a personal refinement of colour and is more melancholy than aggressive. Caravaggio's influence is felt dramatically in the work of

Jusepe de **Ribera** (1591(?)-1652), a Spaniard who worked chiefly at Naples. The mourning figures emerge from a black gloom round the outstretched body of Christ in his *Lamentation* [235]: a deep night of despair, broken only by the shaft of powerful light that blazes over the corpse.

Rome was the adopted home of Adam **Elsheimer** (1578-1610), a German artist whose small landscapes are also something of a revolution. They were to influence such great painters as Rubens (Room XIV) and Claude (Room XX). So small are Elsheimer's pictures that they are easily missed—and not very easy to see. The *Shipwreck of S. Paul* [3535] is a miniature baroque drama, a night piece with effects of stormy light and the excitement of the raging sea splashing high amid the tangled trees. If that picture is Caravaggesque, the *Baptism of Christ* [3904] is calmer and more Venetian, with its brilliant colour and ring of dancing angels. The *Martyrdom of S. Laurence* [1014] seems to unite the two influences of Rome and Venice, and yet it remains Northern in its pre-occupation with detail. The whole small surface is embroidered, as it were, with observation, and pulsating with Elsheimer's touch which give a sort of eerie life to the distant trees—their foliage just touched in—and the sparks from the fire being prepared for the saint. In all three pictures Elsheimer's landscape interest is present, but it swells in the *Tobias and the Angel* [1424] to new proportions. It virtually *is* the subject in this late picture which must date from only shortly before the painter's premature death. The light is lyrical in the distance, gradually diminishing as the trees grow thicker about the dark lake: one peers into the mysterious depths of an intensely poetic, tranquil landscape.

The other great 17th century painter represented in the Room is **Guercino** (1591-1666) who came from Cento, near Bologna, and worked only briefly at Rome. His Venetian-like response to colour and texture is shown on a large scale in the *Incredulity of S. Thomas* [3216], painted in his early style about 1620. This has its own drama but it is poignant in its simplicity: the risen Saviour yields up, with tenderness, his body to the saint's exploratory fingers. The paint is richly applied, richly coloured, giving a satisfying—almost juicy—sense of bulk to the figures and their thickly-folded draperies. In Guercino's small picture *Angels weeping over the dead Christ* [22] the same subtle emotional and tonal sensitivity are combined; the angels do not gesticulate hysterically but kneel in a sort of grieving quiescence, while Christ's body lies in a pose that might almost be that of sleep. The last great Bolognese painter Giuseppe Maria **Crespi** (1665-1747) carries Guercino's sensitivity to colour and atmosphere into the 18th century. His *S. Jerome* [6345] is a harmony of dusky colours, where the saint sits meditating profoundly in a green twilit wilderness.

ROOM XVIIB:

ITALIAN SEVENTEENTH CENTURY

Landscape as a subject for pictures developed fully in the
17th century, partly under the impulse given by Elsheimer
(Room XVIIA). Annibale **Carracci** (1560-1609) was
another great pioneer, and something of his feeling for the
pagan, natural, world—a country world of the classical past
—is apparent in the panels of *Bacchus* (?) *and Silenus* [94]
and *Silenus gathering grapes* [93] which once decorated the
lid of a harpsichord. Both panels have tremendous verve
and gaiety. They seem to evoke, light heartedly, a mood of
rustic freedom. This Room also shows some of the later
achievements of the century by Italian and French painters
chiefly in Rome. The tall *Storm: Moses and the Angel* (?)
[1159] is by Gaspard **Dughet** (1615-1675), the brother-in-
law of Poussin, and like him a Frenchman working in Rome.
The figures hardly matter in this grand and wild scene of
nature at its most savage. It is an Italian landscape luridly
lit and agitated by the elements. Dughet even paints the
driving rain. There is probably no specific subject illustrated by the even more dramatic elemental *Mountain
Landscape* [5593] by the short-lived Francisque **Millet**
(1642-1679). A flash of lightning terrifies the people on the
mountain top and is about to strike in the valley below. One
can almost taste the acrid oppressive air, like thundery
smoke, which darkens the whole scene as the storm rolls
round.

The pictures of **Claude** (1600-1682) are much calmer.
His large-scale work is represented nearby in Room XX,
but three of his earlier small pictures here reveal the lyrical
directness of his response to natural scenery. An actual
topographical scene like the *View in Rome* [1319] is very

unusual with him, but is a reminder that, though he was French, Rome was his home for all his active lifetime. The *Landscape* [58] is of enchanting spontaneity and tranquillity. It has all the sense of a hot summer day in the country, with the goatherd seated piping in the shadows, and a thin stream falling coolly between the sinuous tree trunks. Its calm pastoral mood seems to sum up all that Italy meant to the artist. From a few years later dates the equally small *Landscape with Hagar and the Angel* [61], a more formalised composition, but bathed in cool mists which lie over the water and lend an enchanted unreality to the distant hills. Everything seems contained within one atmospheric envelope. Claude's *Hagar* was inspired in composition by a painting of the Bolognese artist **Domenichino** (1581-1641), which by chance is also in the Gallery: *Landscape with Tobias and the Angel* [48]. This is much earlier than Claude's picture and shows the pioneering aspect of Domenichino as a landscape painter in Italy. The frescoes by Domenichino [6284-90] depict classical subjects from the story of Apollo, set in poetic landscapes; the series comes from Villa Aldobrandini, near Rome, and reveals Domenichino's response to the past and also to the countryside of Italy, re-arranged here for decorative effect. More formal than Elsheimer's scenes, Domenichino's art has its own vein of limpid poetry. In the *S. George and the Dragon* [75] he presents a whole panorama of water, buildings and mountains which stretch like a screen—a very carefully composed one—behind the foreground figures. Domenichino's simple depiction of *Tobias* may be contrasted with the large *Landscape* [6298], of the same subject, by Salvator **Rosa** (1615-73). It is in a landscape of great grandeur and wildness that the angel directs Tobias to catch the fish whose liver and gall will cure his father's blindness. Nature here is not so much re-arranged in the interests of formality as enjoyed for its romantic excesses. The steep rocks, the rush of water, the broken shafts of trees are almost emotionally depicted.

There is a romantic feeling of a different kind to be found in the work of Nicolas **Poussin** (1594 ?-1665). His early pictures have a wild, pagan quality and a thundery light. The so-called *Bacchanal* [39] shows a child, who might be the infant Bacchus, being nursed on wine by satyrs. Light glitters metallically on the foliage and, though some of the darkness is due to the picture's being unfinished, the effect was obviously always meant to be atmospherically dramatic. In *Cephalus and Aurora* [65], a picture of approximately the same date, *i.e.* about 1630, the Sun's chariot is shown rising in the sky, while earth is still shadowy. There is an almost irrational poetry in the sleeping river god, the beautiful white Pegasus, and the reclining goddess at the left who watches the sun rise. As day begins, Cephalus turns away from the restraining arms of Aurora, to gaze on the portrait of his first love, Procris. And Poussin wonderfully suggests the whole world stirring into consciousness again after night.

ROOM XVIIC:

ITALIAN SEVENTEENTH CENTURY

This Room shows some further aspects of painting in 17th century Italy, and is concerned particularly with religious pictures from the schools of Bologna and Naples. The huge *Adoration of the Shepherds* [6270] is by the Bolognese artist Guido **Reni** (1575-1642) and is the only example the Gallery possesses of a Baroque altarpiece. It was commissioned from Reni late in his life by the Prince of Liechtenstein, and shows the light tones and light, almost pencilled, handling typical of Reni's late works. It is meant to dominate from a distance rather than be examined at close range. Then its delicate drama of illumination would make its full effect: a soft night atmosphere brightened by the angels flying over the stable and, more strongly, by the radiant Christ Child who literally illumines the figures who have come to worship Him. Reni's earlier work is represented on a much smaller scale by the highly finished, enamel-smooth, *Coronation of the Virgin* [214], painted on copper. It shows the influence of the Carracci and when it was painted Annibale **Carracci** (1560-1609) was probably still alive, though ill and unable to work. One of Annibale's late pictures is the *Pietà* [2923], with its powerful colour and plangent emotion. The subject was often painted by Annibale but the present picture is, if not the latest, the most intense in its sense of shock and grief. The livid collapsed corpse of Christ is echoed by the fainting figure of the blue and violet-clad Virgin. This extreme movement is checked by the pose of the Mary who supports their two bodies, and balanced by the gesticulating two Marys whose grief almost becomes audible in its piercing tone.

A less intense feeling is communicated in the decorative

pictures of the Neapolitan Luca **Giordano** (1632-1705) whose work is shown on the opposite wall. The so-called *Betrothal* [1434] is a piece of pure fantasy decoration, and in its costumes a homage to Velazquez. Giordano worked all over Italy and eventually also in Spain. At Madrid he executed a series of frescoes of the life of S. Anthony for the church of San Antonio de los Portugeses and the *Miracle of S. Anthony* [1844] is one of his preparatory sketches for these frescoes. Giordano's accomplished handling and brilliance of colour are apparent, even in this patently hasty picture—probably a working sketch for himself. It may be compared with the more solidly handled, more colouristically brilliant, *Martyrdom of S. Januarius* [6327] which is a finished sketch—the *modello*—for Giordano's altarpiece in S. Spirito dei Napoletani, the church of his compatriots in Rome. The altarpiece must have been painted at least by 1692, when Giordano went to Spain. The composition shows the patron saint of Naples, S. Januarius, to whom an angel dramatically appears at the moment of his martyrdom. Heaven and earth are miraculously brought together in a typical instant of Baroque drama. All three pictures reveal Giordano's gifts as decorator and colourist, with his light palette and rapid touch, and help to explain his importance for the decorative painters of the following century (see the pictures of Pellegrini and Ricci in Room XIII). Another Neapolitan painter, less famous and less long-lived, was Bernardo **Cavallino** (1616-1654/6) whose very individual art is seen in the dusky *Christ expelling money-changers from the Temple* [4778] and in the *Finding of Moses* [6297]. Both pictures show the subtlety of his colour-schemes and the almost dancing elegance of his tall figures. Cavallino was an admirer of the great 16th century Venetian painters, and also of Rubens; from these sources he blended his own personal style.

Other painters also fused their style from similar combinations. Bernardo **Strozzi** (1581-1644) moved from his native Genoa—where Rubens had worked—and settled at

Venice. There he must have painted his richly-coloured *Allegorical Figure of Fame* [6321] where the paint is thickly applied with vigorous impasto. This too preludes achievements in 18th century Venice, as does also the work of a German Johann **Liss** (*ca.* 1590-1629) who settled and died in Venice. His *Judith and Holofernes* [4597]—one version of a design he repeated often—shows something of the same combination of Northern and Italian elements. Just as with Cavallino, the result is highly personal and original.

ROOM XVIID:

ITALIAN SIXTEENTH CENTURY

The pictures in this room come from two provincial cities, Ferrara and Brescia, which produced their own highly personal Renaissance styles of painting. The large altarpiece of the *Nativity with Saints* [297] by Gerolamo **Romanino** (born, c. 1484-7; still alive 1559) is full of almost eccentric feeling: with its strangely excited cloud of *putti* and the extreme Giorgionesque grace of the romantic sainted warrior S. Alessandro at the left who yearns towards the central Nativity. The picture comes from the Church of S. Alessandro at Brescia, but more typical of Brescian reality and grasp on humanity are pictures like the richly dressed *Young Man* [299] by **Moretto** (c. 1498-1554) and the sober *Man* (*'The Tailor'*) [697] by Giovan Battista **Moroni** (active 1546-7; d. 1578). Moretto's noble sitter is in himself a whole wardrobe of silks and fur and feather, an opulent Renaissance figure comparable to Jean de Dinteville in Holbein's *Ambassadors* (Room IX). Moroni's *Tailor* is not only less flamboyant but perhaps more sensitively painted. The simple pose is memorably effective and intimate. The tailor is separated from us by no more than the narrow slice of table top, almost a counter, and his glance seems to refer to the spectator as he stands about to cut the cloth.

Ferrara produced very different artists, among them Lorenzo **Costa** (1459/60-1535) whose altarpiece of the *Virgin and Child with Saints* [629] is signed and dated on the throne 1505. Its grave beauty is blended from two styles: in one way looking back to the 15th century (as in the piping child angel and the landscape beyond), and in another looking forward to the suave graces of the new century, especially those of Correggio. An earlier picture by Costa is the *Concert* [2486] where the figures are as hard and clear and bright-coloured as if carved from polished wood. The painter makes almost mathematically abstract shapes out of the musical instruments and the people themselves, with their crab-like hands which clutch at the parapet. The harmony of the voices is carefully observed; each mouth is open, sounding a different note. The picture presents us with the most civilized aspect of the Renaissance, without religious or dynastic preoccupations. Three people come together to sing, and this private concert makes the painter's subject.

Another Ferrarese painter, **Garofalo** (1481(?)-1559) is almost too well represented in the Gallery. His *Pagan Sacrifice* [3928] and *Allegory of Love* [1362] pay tribute to the continuing Renaissance interest in the classical past—but with Garofalo it is hardly more than a last uninspired gasp.

ROOM XVIII:

SPANISH

Within this single room some three centuries of Spanish painting are represented. The emphasis is on the great artists of the 17th century, on above all Diego **Velazquez** (1599-1660). The *Rokeby Venus* [2057], so-called because it was once at Rokeby in Yorkshire, is a unique surviving picture—not only in Velazquez' work but in 17th century Spanish art. The subject of a female nude is otherwise hardly found there. The picture is a tribute to the influence exercised by Venetian art over Velazquez, both in concept and in brushwork. But the result is personal to Velazquez alone. Despite the kneeling cupid who holds the mirror, it is hardly a mythological picture. An almost 'modern' simplicity and directness present us with this profile of a woman's body lying along a bed, the grey-blue silk coverings of which are painted with such breadth and assurance. Velazquez's attachment to reality is already revealed in the early interior of *Christ in the house of Martha and Mary* [1375], where the religious subject is relegated to the background and the picture is really of a kitchen girl and a sparse still-life. In the same way Velazquez' *S. John on Patmos* [6264], another early picture from the painter's youth in Seville, is less a religious picture than the portrait of a young Spaniard. The paint is applied thickly, richly modelling the shape of the face and the heavy folds of the clothes; the saint is very much more firmly present than the rather perfunctory tiny vision which he witnesses. Velazquez' response to recording things as they are remains just as intense when he becomes the portraitist of his king. The full-length *Philip IV of Spain in brown and silver* [1129] shows the king in a costume of unusual splendour, though we know that the king liked to wear brown when not dressed in plain black. It is also rather unusual in being signed by Velazquez—on the paper held in the king's hand. An almost naive effect is given by the shape of the white-stockinged legs against the floor, but the hat lying on the table is painted with a directness that anticipates Manet and Impressionism. The embroidery of the king's costume is indicated by rapid, brilliantly free, brushstrokes—an advance on the heavier handling of his earlier work. No flattery softens Velazquez's eye as paint creates the pale heavy face of the king, and the pale, lifeless, fair hair. This is a portrait of Philip still young. It can be compared with the bust-length *Philip IV* [745], dating from some twenty-five years later. Here the black dress and gold chain—from which hangs the badge of the Golden Fleece—are suitably restrained, muted in importance when compared to the painting of the face in which pink paint seems to create the effect of real flesh, and the complexion's colour infuses the lank hair with faintly pinkish tone. There is no drawing but simply pure painting: paint creates the drooping eyelids, the sagging chin, the myopic eyes. The features are almost dissolving in paint—blurred as if through a veil.

Francisco de **Zurbaran** (1598-1664) was influenced by Velazquez but his best pictures, like the *S. Margaret* [1930], have a personal, almost rustic, realism. S. Margaret is shown as a shepherdess (according to one legend she guarded her nurse's sheep) and carries over one arm saddlebags of a type still seen today in Spain. So solid, serene, and matter of fact does S. Margaret appear that it is a suprise to detect in the background a dragon roaring about her. There is a more emotional quality in Zurbaran's *S. Francis* [5655], but the same strong realisation of textures, as in the saint's worn habit and the ivory smooth bone of the skull he clasps. Like Velazquez, Zurbaran moved from his native Seville to Madrid. Bartholomé Estebán **Murillo** (1617-1682) spent most of his life settled at Seville. His art is much more deliberately decorative than that of either of his great contemporaries. The *Two Trinities* [13] is a cloudy vision of brightly-coloured draperies, culminating in the softly painted, blessing, God the Father who looks down on the earthly Trinity of his Son with Mary and Joseph. The gentle piety of the picture is only one aspect of Murillo's art which is seen in more forceful style in *Christ at the Pool of Bethesda* [5931] and in more pungently realistic style in the impressive *Self Portrait* [6153] which was painted—as the inscription tells—at the wish of the artist's children.

Before the 17th century there had already settled in Spain, at Toledo, **El Greco** (1541-1614), a Cretan who had trained in Italy. In Spain his diversely compounded art took on an intensity all its own. A strange lunar landscape is the setting of *The Agony in the Garden* [3476] where a crater cradles the sleeping Apostles, and everything is lit in a flickering cold light as if by magnesium. Tall figures of flame-like, wavering, shape dramatically sway across the composition of *Christ driving the traders from the Temple* [1457], dominated by the tallest figure of all, Christ, who seems almost dancing with energy. Greco's *Adoration of the Name of Jesus* [6260] is probably the preparatory *modello* for his big picture of the subject, painted for Philip II. The king is shown in black kneeling with the Pope and the Doge of Venice. The subject probably originates in the alliance of the Holy League which the three had formed against the Turks. In 1571 the League won a great victory at Lepanto, and it is this perhaps which is allegorised by the picture.

There is little continuity in Spanish art, and from the death of Murillo to the birth of Goya more than sixty years passed unspectacularly. Foreign painters served Spain, and under their influence Francisco de **Goya** (1746-1828) painted his early pictures. His attractive colour and decorative treatment of genre is shown in the sketch for a tapestry cartoon, *A Picnic* [1471], probably painted in the 1780's. As well as this charming sort of picture, Goya was also concerned with more irrational aspects of human nature. Witchcraft stands for him as a black side of nature; but as we see it in *A Scene*

CLAUDE   LANDSCAPE: HAGAR AND THE ANGEL
                            ROOM XVIIB

VELAZQUEZ

PHILIP IV OF SPAIN
ROOM XVIII

from 'El Hechizado por Fuerza' [1472] the bewitchment is only comic. The subject is taken from a play where a frightened man believes that his life will last only as long as a lamp remains alight. He is shown desperately filling the lamp, while a grotesque picture of a dance of donkeys adds to his fright. Goya is also a great portrait painter. A Velazquez-like freedom of handling marks the silvery portrait of *Dr. Peral* [1951] where the clothes almost ripple in their watery, subtle tones. Dr. Peral is said to have been a financial representative of the Spanish government, but his face does not give one much confidence in his probity. Just as Goya pitilessly records those features so he equally vividly, but more attractively, records the appearance of *Doña Isabel Cobos de Porcel* [1473]. She wears the showy lower class costume of a *maja* which was often assumed by fashionable women. Indeed, the picture's flaunting 'Spanishness' has an element of dressing up in it, but the bold air of the picture really comes from the confident sitter herself and the artist's response to her.

ROOM XIX:

FRENCH EIGHTEENTH CENTURY

The 18th century French pictures in this room are hardly more than a token representation of a great period in French art, and being all on a small scale they cannot suggest its big decorative achievements. To appreciate the full splendours of French 18th century art, and the whole decorative ensemble it created, one must go to the Wallace Collection. Grace and charm are early declared in Antoine **Watteau** (1684-1721), but there is much more to his work. *La Gamme d'Amour* [2897] captures a moment of love as the singer turns to her accompanist and the song is interrupted by their exchange of glances. With Watteau music is always the food of love. Yet the mood has something of sunset sadness. There is a suggestion of the transitoriness of human feelings, perhaps emphasised by the bust that seems already to have survived so long, that will be still enduring stone when the human presences beneath it have crumbled away. A delicate, almost musical, range of colour is manipulated by Watteau in tones of warm bronze and russet and gleaming mauveish-pink, evanescent, subtle colours which are at once sweet and sad. The whole painting is delicate and yet strong—how strong is revealed by the slight, light-hearted, pictures of Nicolas **Lancret** (1690-1743) whose two series of pictures *The Four Ages of Man* [101-104] and *The Four Times of the Day* [5867-5870] are prettified genre. They aim almost too obviously at pleasing, but their sheer charm is irresistible. They emphasise the attractive aspects of life in 18th century France, and the portraits of the period also woo the spectator by their appealing charm. People take on the bloom and fragility of porcelain, becoming themselves objets d'art.

Through the medium of pastel, a particular enchantment is given to portraits like the *Girl with a Cat* [3588]—a harmony in blue—by Jean-Baptiste **Perronneau** (1715 ?-1783). The greatest of these pastel artists was Maurice-Quentin de **La Tour** (1704-1788) who is represented only by the rather unexciting *Henry Dawkins* [5118]. The most sheerly charming of all the portraits in the Room is that of *Manon Balletti* [5586] by the fashionable court painter Jean-Marc **Nattier** (1685-1766). It is signed and dated 1757 and shows the young sitter just at the period she became engaged to Casanova whom, perhaps fortunately, she did not finally marry. Here the charm is directly the sitter's own; the painter has no need to flatter but instead captures an unaffected, half-smiling grace which seems so much part of the personality of Manon Balletti.

Amid the charming and the pretty, the work of Jean-Baptiste-Siméon **Chardin** (1699-1779), asserts a more rigorous and intellectual note, even while reflecting daily life. *The Young Schoolmistress* [4077], one version of several of this composition, shows Chardin's dignified, even didactic, art in which every object has its mathematical place in the composition, and is painted with intense conviction. Chardin's people are usually simple, and never quite idle; here a child gravely teaches another child. In the *House of Cards* [4078] the boy concentrates so seriously that cardbuilding almost ceases to be a game. These are pictures in which humble genre is treated with the high seriousness of Poussin. After these domestic interiors one can turn to the picture of *A Street Show in Paris* [2129], by Gabriel de **Saint-Aubin** (1724-80) which hangs just outside Room XIX. Saint-Aubin's paintings are not common, and this lively, charming, picture gives an attractive view of people enjoying themselves in a Parisian boulevard in the middle years of the 18th century.

ROOM XX:

FRENCH SEVENTEENTH CENTURY

The majority of pictures in this Room were painted not in France but in Rome. There lived the two greatest French painters of the 17th century, Claude Lorraine and Poussin who are recorded as friends. In the last year of Poussin's life there is a vivid reference to him as no longer doing much except sometimes taking a glass of wine with his neighbour Claude. But as painters they have little in common. **Claude** (1600-1682) paints nothing but landscapes and seascapes, part factual, part imaginary. Though the figures are small in these pictures, the stories depicted are often carefully worked out and the variations of mood and time of day give their variety to pictures which look the same only at first glance. There is a whole group of pictures dating from the 1640's: the pastoral of *Cephalus and Procris* [27] where cattle ford the stream oblivious of the mythological figures at the right; the large *Marriage of Isaac and Rebekah* ('*The Mill*') [12]; and the two Seaport scenes, [5 and 14], the latter an early morning scene with the *Embarkation of the Queen of Sheba*. The first rays of sun glitter on the water and, as the Queen of Sheba steps down to the quayside, trumpeters sound from the high balcony above her. All these pictures entered the Gallery at its founding in 1824, with the purchase of the Angerstein collection. Perhaps even more impressive than any of these is the large and later *David at the Cave of Adullam* [6], with its panorama of countryside and its tall crystalline mountains which melt into the white horizon; in this setting David is shown refusing to drink the water which three heroes have brought him from the cistern at Bethlehem in the Philistines' camp—seen at the left. A much later picture still is *Æneas at Delos* [1018], dated 1672. Here the figures have become very tall and slender, suitable inhabitants of the strange, highly personalised, somewhat shaky world which is that of Claude's last paintings. The white-robed king points out to Aeneas, and his father and son, the sights of Delos—the island where Apollo was born. They have recently landed on the island and theirs are the boats anchored in the misty blue sea which so gently washes the coast of an ideal country.

Classical subjects are treated in a much less nostalgic way by Nicolas **Poussin** (1594 ?-1665). And in his pictures the human figure regains its full importance. The large imposing *Adoration of the Golden Calf* [5597], is a composition like a frieze with its interwoven dancing figures at the left united to the adoring group at the right by the white-robed Aaron. Some of the dancing figures occur in reverse in the bibulous *Bacchanalian Revel* [62]. Here Poussin's own poetry, a poetry of imagination combined with intellect, is seen at its most typical. There is tremendous animation and Venetian high spirits under the carefully organised design: a marble frieze has come to life in this Titianesque countryside of blue mountains and heavily-foliaged trees. Venetian painting meant a great deal to Poussin. His later pictures impose order on wildness and irrationality. Nature is already ordered and rearranged to some extent in the two small *Landscapes in the Campagna* (loaned to the Gallery), looking forward to the great organised panorama of the *Landscape with a Snake* [5763]. This was finished in 1648 for Poussin's friend, the banker Pointel, and is the first of the painter's grand classical landscapes. The eye is led in serpentine fashion from the dead man in the foreground, through the windings of the landscape, until it comes to rest on the cubist forms of the buildings reflected in the lake. A *frisson* of terror also runs through the composition: from the man who sees the corpse to the woman who, seeing his fright, communicates her fear to the men resting at the lakeside and the boatmen on the water.

The art of Poussin was nourished in Rome: antiquity hovers around all his pictures, whether or not they are classical in subject. His *Adoration of the Shepherds* [6277] may be compared with the *Adoration of the Shepherds* [6331] by a contemporary French artist Louis **Le Nain** (*ca.* 1593-1648). Le Nain had probably been in Italy but there is nothing classical or antique in his treatment. Rather, the Adoration takes place in humble, rustic surroundings and the shepherds are French peasants. Even the two enchanting child angels are—as it were—children dressed up for a Nativity play. Poussin's composition is more noble and elevated; the genre elements are carefully controlled, and the composition ordered against the background of dignified ruins.

Both Poussin and Le Nain represent unofficial aspects of French 17th century art. The consciously humble subject matter of Antoine **Le Nain** (*ca.* 1588-1648), Louis' brother, is part of the appeal in the small interior, *A Woman and Five Children* [1425]. These peasant people sit austerely, a little stiffly, observed with directness and given a touching dignity. There is refreshing realism in this art after the more grandiose aspects of court art in France at the period. Philippe de **Champaigne** (1602-1674) worked for the king and for Cardinal Richelieu whom he also portrayed. The Gallery possesses a full length portrait by him of the Cardinal and also the very interesting *Triple Portrait* [798], which shows Richelieu bust-length in three poses. This was done for a sculptor, and it may well have served for a marble bust now in the Louvre, which was probably executed in the studio of the greatest Italian sculptor of the period, Bernini.

ROOM XXI:

NINETEENTH CENTURY FRENCH

It is no accident that amid so many pictures of simple objects and moments of daily life in this Room there should stand out the large scale *Baignade* [3908] by Georges **Seurat** (1859-1891). Time is suspended and daily life transcended in this, the first of Seurat's large mural-size paintings, executed when the short-lived artist was in his early twenties. Like the Impressionists, Seurat chooses an everyday, ordinary scene. It is a hot Sunday afternoon on the banks of the Seine at Asnières, an industrial suburb of Paris, but time seems to have stopped. The simplified forms seems to take on an eternal aspect, drained of distracting detail. The boy sits forever on the bank in a world of carefully planned, almost geometrical shapes—silhouettes from which life has been sucked to make them become art. Seurat rejected the fleeting moment, and gave monumentality and timelessness to what had originally been genre. He is in this a Chardin, though his technique is very different.

Beside the rigid intellectual scheme of *Une Baignade*, the nearby *Servante de Bocks* [3858], by Edouard **Manet** (1832-1883), is positively pulsating with crowded life, immediate in comparison with the pondered sense of Seurat's picture. Manet's painting is only half of his original composition which was a scene in the brasserie de Reichshoffen at Paris. The picture was painted in the late 1870's—at which time waitresses were comparatively new in brasseries—and shows Manet's direct handling of paint in high tones. Paint makes the forms and is handled in a more daring way than in the much earlier *Musique Aux Tuileries* [3260] which also presents a more decorous society. But it remains a brilliant glimpse of Second Empire life and of a scene visited almost daily by Manet and his friend Baudelaire. Both of them are included among the many portraits in the picture. Manet made studies in the open air on the spot and the picture retains this sense of light and air vividly set down on canvas. Manet aimed also at the depiction of contemporary events. He painted several versions of the *Execution of the Emperor Maximilian* and the Gallery owns some fragments from one of these, including the *Firing Party* [3294A] and a *Soldier* [3294B]. The unfortunate Maximilian had been imprudently elected emperor of Mexico, under French pressure, and was shot by the Mexicans in 1867. The incident created a sensation in Europe and Manet seems to have been guided by newspaper reports, as well as photographs of the scene. By choosing such a subject Manet showed the painter's willingness to share in the life of his period, to be—to some extent—'engaged'. A 'history' picture is no longer concerned with classical or mythological people but with contemporary life and with a shocking incident.

Manet was at first regarded as the leader of the revolutionary group of Impressionists. Perhaps more deeply Impressionist, and certainly less concerned with aspects of daily life, was Claude-Oscar **Monet** (1840-1926) who is represented most typically in Room XXII but whose small early *Beach at Trouville* [3951] shows the *plein air* directness and spontaneity so much sought by the group. Pierre-Auguste **Renoir** (1841-1919) was closely associated with Impressionism and *La Première Sortie* [3859] dates from about the period of Manet's *Servante de Bocks*. Renoir's is a rainbow impressionism, catching the warm brilliance of a theatre and the excitement of the child's first visit. The paint caresses the canvas, conveying the bloom of skin and the texture of clothes. Renoir was soon to dispense with the clothes and to paint chiefly the nude. *La Source* [5982] is a large-scale example and the small *Baigneuse se Coiffant* [6319] shows his ravishing response to flesh in sunlight and open air. The form is rapidly, sensuously modelled and set amid feathery, flecked, greenery which serves to set off the peach tones of the body.

Camille **Pissarro** (1830-1903) was also an Impressionist painter, one whose chief interest was not in figure painting but in landscape. A comparatively early work is the *View from Louveciennes* [3265] which has a direct spring-like air and simplicity in concept and technique. The urban view of Paris, *The Boulevard Montmartre at Night* [4119] shows how much freer and more truly impressionistic Pissarro's handling had become by this date of 1897. In that year Pissarro took a room in a hotel near the Boulevard Montmartre and painted several views of it. This picture seems to be the only one showing it by night, and the very sketchy technique well conveys the effect of buildings lit by flaring gaslight. Pissarro was particularly to influence Paul **Cézanne** (1839-1906) whose own art was much tougher and more constructed than most Impressionist painting. The artist himself confronts us in the small but concentrated image of *Cézanne chauve* [4135] where effective use is made of the wallpaper pattern in the background. Cézanne's portraits are few, but the same concentrated power is found in the *Vieille au Chapelet* [6195]—the portrait of an old ex-servant who must have posed long for this worked and re-worked canvas. The final result is almost hacked out of the paint. Cézanne's landscapes reveal how far he was from resting content with the 'impression' of a scene. The *Aix: Paysage Rocheux* [4136] powerfully models, with nearly cubist effect, a stretch of rocky roadside in the country around Cézanne's own birthplace. This is the landscape he had known all his life and which he was to depict again and again, seeking to capture the exact sensations that he had before it. In his late paintings nature provides merely the scaffolding for him to clothe with personal shapes and colour. *Dans le Parc du Château Noir* [6342] is glowing with strange blues and blacks like a leaded stained-glass window. Out of the tall tree trunks Cézanne makes a mesh of almost abstract shapes, growing out of the excitingly tilted plane of the ground. The reality of the wooded park of a Provençal château has been transfigured into a work of art which anticipates the development of Cubism in the twentieth century. It is symbolically right that the picture should have been painted probably about 1900.

ROOM XXII:

FRENCH NINETEENTH CENTURY

The pictures in this Room carry one on into modern times, just as some of the painters themselves carried on to survive into a period very changed after the cataclysm of the first world war. And when Monet died in 1926 Matisse was already in his fifties and Picasso in his forties. Monet's very last pictures were the series of *Nymphéas*, or Water-lilies, studies on a large scale of a section of his water-garden at Giverny. An early view of this is provided in the *Bassin aux Nymphéas* [4240], which is of 1899. In this is also included the Japanese-style bridge, built by Monet, and the trees overhanging the pond. In the late *Water Lilies* [6343] reality has receded further. Only the water, with a few plants on it, is the subject: a vast shimmering surface which reflects and also reveals, so that the eye can hardly distinguish what is growing in the water from what it mirrors. Monet remains true to the principle of painting what he sees. But in his last years his eyesight was tragically failing and eventually he was operated on for cataract in 1923. It is perhaps oncoming cataract which explains the sulphur-yellow tone which predominates in the *Water Lilies* and which is also part of its fascination. Traditional vision, tonality, technique, are all exchanged for the creation of a picture which virtually has no subject but paint and colour. More than a pond, it is a mood which is evoked, and into which the spectator must plunge for his enjoyment.

While Monet never departed from the principles of Impressionism, Renoir was to move increasingly towards a monumental but highly personal classicism in which woman is the chief subject. The two tall decorative canvases of *Danseuses* [6317-8] were painted in 1909 for the dining room of a Parisian apartment. They well show the broad forms and handling Renoir had evolved at this period, and they have a full-blown, autumnal sensuousness. Hot flesh and exotic draperies are caressed by the brush of the ageing crippled painter whose joy in his art animates the two pictures.

Although he exhibited with the Impressionists, Hilaire-Germain-Edgar **Degas** (1834-1917) can be claimed to be very different in technique and in his artistic aims. He was the only great 19th century painter to be influenced by Ingres. Superb, acid draughtsmanship is the essence of his style. His subject, however, is usually contemporary life: the circus, the races, the ballet. The *Jeunes Spartiates* [3860] is an unfinished picture of a classical subject—the fights between boys and girls in ancient Sparta. It pays tribute to the literacy of Degas who not only read classical authors but himself possessed an incisive command of language. For Degas the scene becomes a study of so many bodies in action; and he was to study the same subject in more intimate, and contemporary, surroundings. Moments of action are seized on vividly by him—with deliberate, almost camera, effects like that of *La La at the Cirque Fernando* [4121]. Here the brilliantly unexpected angle conveys the dizzy feeling of watching the acrobat swinging in space as she is raised on the wire by her teeth. The steep angle is emphasised by the diagonal of the taut wire and by the arches and struts of the circus roof, as well as by the foreshortened figure of La La herself, a mulatto who performed feats of strength. If one looks up at her, then one looks down at the pattern of bodies on the sand in the enchanting *Bains de Mer* [3247] where a girl lies having her hair combed by her nurse. Degas' use of line is always as taut as wire, keen and often positively witty; here the shape made by the drying bathing dress has the same quality of wit as the huddled shapes of the wrapped-up bathers at the sea's edge. And for all its suggestions of plein-air, the picture was painted in Degas' studio. The much larger *Combing the*

Hair [4865] is a later picture, perhaps not totally finished, and perhaps not totally successful. But it represents Degas' increasing concern with isolating moments of ordinary, indeed intimate, life. Again and again he was to study women at their toilet, with a fascination that is almost cruel in its intensity. The goddess-women of Ingres are now seen to move, strip, wash, and comb out their long hair, as if oblivious of any spectator.

The Gallery possesses only a few pictures to convey the greatness of Vincent van **Gogh** (1853-1890). The *Cornfield and Cypress trees* [3861] was painted in the penultimate year of his life, at St. Rémy in Provence. It reveals a very different approach to landscape painting from that of either the Impressionists or Cézanne. Here Van Gogh's vision is partly a linear one; and the cornfield, the trees, the clouds, are all agitated in rolling, curving lines. The cypresses quiver like dark green flames—and van Gogh was obsessed by them as he had the year before been obsessed by sunflowers. The *Sunflowers* [3863] is one of seven pictures of the subject painted by the artist. He intended these pictures to be decorations, at first for his own studio at Arles. Van Gogh himself spoke of 'the sort of effect of Gothic stained glass windows' in the brilliant tones of yellow and orange which make the picture blaze on the wall. Each flower is like a miniature sun of hot flaring colour, together symbolising a brief moment of joy in the painter's life.

ROOM XXIII:

FRENCH NINETEENTH CENTURY

This Room reveals other aspects of art in 19th century France apart from the perhaps over-familiar Impressionist and Post-Impressionist movements. It serves as reminder of the historical climate, particularly in the mid-century, and as reminder too of the rival artistic aims of two great painters, Ingres and Delacroix. While Ingres studied under David, Delacroix was to be influenced by the stormy revolutionary art of Jean-Louis-André-Théodore **Géricault** (1791-1824) with its dramatic emphasis on realism. Géricault's *Horse frightened by Lightning* [4927] gives some flavour of his dramatic effects and romantic pursuit of sensation, as well as conveying something of his bravura handling of paint. Jean-Auguste-Dominique **Ingres** (1780-1867) stands for the conservative standards of line and design, and also for that academicism which Impressionism was to destroy. The final waxen flower of Ingres' art, and its justification, is in *Madame Moitessier seated* [4821], a picture on which he laboured for some twelve years, completing it in 1856 at the age of seventy-six. Here in an intricate world of metal and fringes and embroidery, Madame Moitessier and her perfect profile sit forever reflected in a series of chilly mirrors. All the wealth of an industrial age has gone to adorn this ample woman who is at once commonplace and yet a goddess—a sphinx of soapstone, without a secret. Ingres himself dressed and undressed this portrait, changed its clothes and shifted the jewellery until he achieved the exact, confident and complete image he desired. Ultimately, thanks to Ingres, Madame Moitessier triumphs, vacuous but supreme, even over the elaborate pattern of her dress and the detailed recordings of her surroundings. Despite some damage, Ingres' *Monsieur de Norvins* [3291] shows how impressively the artist could also record male sitters and how he always responded to the details of costume as much as physiognomy. The smaller pictures by Ingres include the tiny *Oedipus and the Sphinx* [3290] where the artist's response to antiquity goes beyond subject and the pose of Oedipus; the composition is as carefully chiselled as if to give the effect of some antique cameo.

Almost like an answer to the elaborate refinement of *Madame Moitessier* is the full-length portrait of *Baron Schwiter* [3286] by Ferdinand-Victor Eugène **Delacroix** (1798-1863). Schwiter was himself a painter, as well as a distinguished collector, and a friend of Delacroix's. The portrait dates from 1826 when Delacroix was still young and the sitter only twenty-one. It is a fully romantic portrait, both in its glossy handling of paint and in Delacroix's concept of his dandified sitter. It was refused at the Salon exhibition of 1827, a symbol of the refusal of more conservative opinion to accept Delacroix's work with its ranging audacious colour and brushwork. A much later picture, *Ovid among the Scythians* [6262], was exhibited at the Salon in 1859 but was badly received by most critics—except Baudelaire. He vehemently praised the picture as one particularly appealing to poetic temperaments, and spoke of the way the eye can sink into the picture, perhaps attracted by the lake and the distant vigorously-handled shapes of the mountains that recede towards an equally vigorously painted sky with its scumbled, modelled clouds. It is the open air that provides the theme and inspiration for Louis-Eugène **Boudin** (1824-1898) who painted chiefly seascapes in Normandy. His two scenes of the Beach at *Trouville* [6309, 6310] once belonged to Monet, whom Boudin considerably influenced. From these, and the third picture of the same scene [6312], can be traced the evolution of Monet whose own *Beach at Trouville* is in Room XXI. Before Boudin was born there was already active the father of landscape painting in 19th century France, Jean-Baptiste-Camille **Corot** (1796-1875), whose small and early *Roman Campagna with the Claudian Aqueduct* [3285] has a directness and clear-eyed vision which is revolutionary. It captures also something of the artist's own simplicity of character. Corot's views of his native land share this effective simplicity; the subject need be no more than morning light in a country lane, as in the *Dardagny View* [6339] or the very late *La Charette* [6340] which is dated 1874.

Somewhat isolated from all these developments, Ignace-Henri-Jean-Théodore **Fantin-Latour** (1836-1904) specialised in flower painting. There is a Victorian opulence about his basket of *Roses* [3726] with its range of creamy colours and overblown velvet petals. Even richer and more colourful is '*The Rosy Wealth of June*' [1686]: such was the artist's own title for this vase heavy with summer flowers. The effect is almost too virtuoso in its suggestions of the texture and even scent of the different blooms; but Fantin still manages to make art out of subjects which offer a dangerous temptation of prettiness to the painter.

The visitor will pass other, more prickly, flowers in crossing back through Room XXII to leave the Gallery: those brilliant writhing *Sunflowers* of Van Gogh's, painted with deliberate simplicity, and concerned with something more profound than surface appearance. That picture breaks most of the rules on which until then Western Art had been based. And although it now hangs in the National Gallery, it and its creator found no appreciation during his lifetime. It stands like a beacon of yellow fire, reminding us that outside the museum art is always evolving. We have only to look.

GOYA   DOÑA ISABEL COBOS DE PORCEL

ROOM XVIII

CÉZANNE

DANS LE PARC DU CHATEAU NOIR
ROOM XXI

A BRIEF HISTORICAL SUMMARY

The National Gallery was founded in 1824, when Parliament voted £60,000 for the purchase, preservation and exhibition of the greater part of the collection of the late John Julius Angerstein. These thirty-eight pictures included five by Claude and the six of Hogarth's series *Marriage à la Mode*. Other pictures were soon added. In 1826 Titian's *Bacchus and Ariadne* was bought and Sir George Beaumont gave his collection, which included Rubens' *Château de Steen* and Canaletto's *The Stone-Mason's Yard*. The Holwell Carr Bequest of 1831 included Tintoretto's *S. George and the Dragon* and Rembrandt's *Woman bathing*.

A consistent policy of acquisition was adopted in 1855, when a regular grant for purchases was first voted in Parliament and the first Director, Sir Charles Eastlake, P.R.A. (d. 1865) was appointed. By the end of the nineteenth century the further pursuit of this policy by his two successors, Sir William Boxall and Sir Frederic Burton, had resulted in what is perhaps the most widely representative collection in the world of the great schools of European painting before 1800.

Considerable additions have been made in this century, several through the National Art-Collections Fund. Important bequests of pictures included those by George Salting (1910), Sir Hugh Lane (1917) and Ludwig Mond (1924). Several generous bequests of money, especially the Temple West Bequest (1907), have been made. The Lane Bequest and a number of purchases, several made with a Fund given by the late Samuel Courtauld, have secured some masterpieces of the French nineteenth century. In 1959 an arrangement was made whereby the Lane Bequest pictures are divided into two parts, each lent alternately for five years to Dublin, over a period of twenty years.

For the first ten years the National Gallery collection was exhibited at Mr. Angerstein's house, 100 Pall Mall, and from 1834 at No. 105. In 1838 it was first exhibited in the present building, constructed in 1834-37 on the site of the King's Mews to the design of William Wilkins. The building was then not more than one Room deep; and it was shared with the Royal Academy, which occupied the Eastern half until 1869. The removal of the Academy in that year to Burlington House and the extension of the National Collection the whole length of the building only emphasised the need for more space. The first extension, to the designs of E. M. Barry, opened in 1876, included the Dome and the adjoining Rooms XVII, A, B, C, D, together with Rooms XIV, XV, and XVI. The second, which gave the Central Staircase its present form and included Rooms XII, XIII, and XIII, A, B, and C, was opened in 1887. Since 1945 several Rooms have been re-modelled and air-conditioned, and this work is still in progress. Room VIII D was destroyed in the war but has been rebuilt, and a new Room—IX—has been added to the Gallery. Further extensions are planned.

British painting was represented in the Collection from the first; but the proportion of British pictures became the larger with the Vernon Gift of 1847 and the bequest in 1851 by J. M. W. Turner of all the pictures, etc., remaining in the artist's possession. In 1897 the Tate Gallery was opened, to house the more modern British pictures. The Turner Bequest was mostly transferred there in 1910, more than two hundred British pictures in 1929 and more than three hundred between 1945 and 1954. Meanwhile, in 1917 the Tate Gallery had become also the National Gallery of Modern Foreign Art and received the Lane Bequest, which has now returned to Trafalgar Square. Though the Tate Gallery has had a separate Board of Trustees and Director since 1917 the National Collection of pictures remained one, vested in the National Gallery Trustees, until the National Gallery and Tate Gallery Act of 1954.

INDEX OF EXHIBITED ARTISTS

Artists are indexed below even when the picture in question may be only attributed or related in general style to their work. In this respect the detailed catalogues of the various schools have been followed.

A

Artist	*Room No.*
ALTDORFER, Albrecht	IX
ANDREA da Firenze	II
ANGELICO, Fra	III
ANTONELLO da Messina	VIIIa
ARENTSZ, Arent	X
AVERCAMP, Hendrick	X

B

BAKHUIZEN, Ludolf	X
BALDOVINETTI, Alesso	VIIIc
BALDUNG, Hans	IX
BARBARI, Jacopo de'	VIIIb
BARTOLO di Fredi	I
BARTOLOMMEO, Fra (Bartolommeo della Porta)	VI
BASAITI, Marco	VIIIb
BASSANO, Jacopo	VII
BELLINI, Gentile	VIIIa, VIIIb
BELLINI, Giovanni	VIIIb
BENOZZO di Lese (called Gozzoli)	III
BERCHEM, Nicolaes	X, XIII
BERCKHEYDE, Gerrit	X, XII
BERGOGNONE, Ambrogio	XIIIa
BERTELOT, Guillaume	XVII

Artist	Room No.
BISSOLO, Francesco	VIIIa
BOL, Ferdinand	XI
BOLTRAFFIO, Giovanni Antonio	XIIIa
BONO da Ferrara	VIIIb
BONSIGNORI, Francesco	VIIIb
BONVIN, François	XXIII
BORCH, Gerard ter	X, XII
BORDONE, Paris	XIIIb
BOSCH, Hieronymus	VIIId
BOTH, Jan	XII
BOTTICELLI, Sandro	III, VIIIc
BOUCHER, François	XIX
BOUDIN, Louis-Eugène	XXIII
BOUTS, Dieric	VIIId
BRAIJ, Jan de	X
BRAMANTINO	XIIIa
BREENBERGH, Bartholomeus	X
BREKELENKAM, Quiringh van	X
BRONZINO	VI
BROUWER, Adriaen	XIV
BRUEGEL, Pieter, the Elder	VIIId
BRUGGHEN, Hendrick ter	X
BRUSSEL, Paulus Theodorus van	X

C

'CAMPIN, Robert'	VIIId
CANALETTO	XIII
CAPPELLE, Jan van de	X, XII
CARAVAGGIO	XVIIa

INDEX OF EXHIBITED ARTISTS

Artist	*Room No.*
CARPACCIO, Vittore	VIIIa
CARRACCI, Annibale	XVIIb, XVIIc
CATENA, Vincenzo	XIIIb
CAVALLINO, Bernardo	XVIIc
CÉZANNE, Paul	XXI
CHAMPAIGNE, Philippe de	XX
CHARDIN, Jean-Baptiste-Siméon	XIX
CHRISTUS, Petrus	VIIId
CIMA da Congeliano, Giovanni Battista	VIIIa, VIIIb
CLAUDE	XVIIb, XX
CODDE, Pieter	X
CONSTABLE, John	XV
COROT, Jean-Baptiste-Camille	XXIII
CORREGGIO	VI
COSSA, Francesco del	VIIIa
COSTA, Lorenzo	XIIIb, XVII, XVIId
COURBET, Jean-Desiré-Gustave	XXI, XXII
CRANACH the Elder, Lucas	IX
CRESPI, Giuseppe Maria	XVIIa
CRIVELLI, Carlo	XIIIc
CUYP, Aelbert	X, XII

D

DAVID, Gerard	VIII, VIIId
DECKER, Cornelis	X
DEGAS, Hilaire-Germain-Edgar	XXI, XXII, XXIII
DELACROIX, Ferdinand-Victor-Eugène	XXIII
DOMENICHINO	XVIIb

Artist	*Room No.*
DOU, Gerrit	X, XI
DUBBELS, Hendrick	X
DUCCIO	I
DUGHET, Gaspard	XVIIb, XX
DÜRER, Albrecht	IX
DUYSTER, Willem	X
DYCK, Sir Anthony van	XIV

E

ELSHEIMER, Adam	XVIIa
EYCK, Jan van	VIIId

F

FABRITIUS, Bernhard	XI
FABRITIUS, Carel	XI
FANTIN-LATOUR, Ignace-Henri-Jean-Théodore	
	XXIII
FIORENZO di Lorenzo	IV
FOPPA, Vincenzo	XIIIa
FRAGONARD, Jean-Honoré	XIX
FRANCESCO di Giorgio	II
FRANCIA, Francesco	XVIII

G

GADDI, Agnolo	II
GAINSBOROUGH, Thomas	XVI
GAROFALO (Benvenuto Tisi)	XVII, XVIId
GAUGUIN, Paul	XXII
GEERTGEN tot Sint Jans	VIIId

INDEX OF EXHIBITED ARTISTS

Artist	*Room No.*
GERICAULT, Jean-Louis-André-Théodore	XXIII
GEROLAMO dai Libri	VIIIa
GÉRÔME, Jean-Léon	XXIII
GHIRLANDAIO, Domenico	VIIIc
GIAMBONO, Michele	I
'GIAMPIETRINO'	XIIIa
GIOLFINO, Niccolò	VIIIb
GIORDANO, Luca	XVIIc
GIORGIONE	VII
GIOTTO	I
GIOVANNI d'Alemagna	I
GIOVANNI da Milano	II
GIOVANNI da Oriolo	VIIIb
'GIOVANNI del Ponte'	II
GIOVANNI di Paolo	II
GIUSTO de' Menabuoi	I
GOGH, Vincent van	XXII
GOSSAERT, Jan, called Mabuse	VIII
GOYA, Francisco de	XVIII
GOYEN, Jan van	X
EL GRECO	XVIII
GREUZE, Jean-Baptiste	XIX
GUARDI, Francesco	XIII
GUERCINO	XVIIa

H

HALS, Dirck	X
HALS, Frans	X
HELST, Bartholomeus van der	XII

Artist	*Room No.*
HEYDEN, Jan van der	X
HOBBEMA, Meyndert	X, XII
HOGARTH, William	XVI
HOLBEIN, Hans, the Younger	IX
HONTHORST, Gerrit van	X
HOPPNER, John	XVI
HOOGH, Pieter de	X, XII
HOOGSTRATEN, Samuel van	X
HUIJSUM, Jan van	X

I

| INGRES, Jean-Auguste-Dominique | XXIII |

J

JACOMETTO Veneziano	VIIIb
JARDIN, Karel du	X
JOOS van Wassenhove	VIII
JORDAENS, Jacob	XIV

K

| KONINCK, Philips. | XI |

L

LA HIRE, Laurent de	XX
LANCRET, Nicolas	XIX
LASTMAN, Pieter	XI
LA TOUR, Maurice-Quentin de	XIX
LAWRENCE, Sir Thomas	XVI

Artist	*Room No.*
LENAIN, 'Antoine'	XX
LENAIN, 'Louis'	XX
LEONARDO da Vinci	V, VI
LÉPINE, Stanislas-Victor-Edmond (?)	XXIII
LE SUEUR, Eustache	XX
LEYSTER, Judith	X
LIPPI, Filippino	IV, VIIIc
LIPPI, Fra Filippo	III
LISS, Johann	XVIIc
LOCHNER, Stefan	IX
LONGHI, Pietro	XIII
LORENZETTI, Ambrogio	I
LORENZETTI, Pietro	I
LORENZO Monaco, Don	II
LOTTO, Lorenzo	XIIIb
LUCAS van Leyden	VIIId
LUINI, Bernardino	XIIIa

M

MAES, Nicolaes	X, XI
MAINERI, Gian Francesco de'	XVII
MANET, Édouard	XXI
MANTEGNA, Andrea	VIIIa
MARGARITO of Arezzo	I
MARINUS van Reymerswaele	VIIId
'MARMION, Simon'	VIIId
MASACCIO	III
MASOLINO	III

Artist	*Room No.*
MASSYS, Quinten	VIII, VIIId
MASTER OF S. BARTHOLOMEW	IX
MASTER of S. GILES	VIIId
MASTER of the View of S. GUDULE	VIIId
MASTER of LIESBORN	IX
MASTER of the LIFE of the Virgin	IX
MASTER of the PALA Sforzesca	XIIIa
MATTEO di Giovanni	IV
MAZO, Juan Bautista del	XVIII
MELONE, Altobello	XVIId
MEMLINC, Hans	VIIId
METSU, Gabriel	X
MICHELANGELO	VI
MIERIS the Elder, Frans van	X
MILLET, Francisque	XVIIb
MOLENAER, Jan	X
MONET, Claude-Oscar	XXI, XXII
MONTAGNA, Bartolomeo	VIIIb
MORANDO, Paolo	VIIIa
MORETTO	XVII, XVIId
MORISOT, Berthe	XXI
MORONE, Domenico	VIIIa
MORONE, Francesco	VIIIa
MORONI, Giambattista	XIIIb, XVIId
MURILLO, Bartolomé Esteban	XVIII

N

NARDO di Cione	II
NATTIER, Jean-Marc	XIX

INDEX OF EXHIBITED ARTISTS

Artist	Room No.
NEER, Aernout (Aert) van der	X, XII
NICCOLÒ di Pietro Gerini	II

O

OLIS, Jan	X
ORCAGNA, Andrea di Cione, called	I, II
ORSI, Lelio	XIIIb
L'ORTOLANO	XVIId
OSTADE, Adriaen van	X
OSTADE, Isack van	X

P

PACHER, Michael	IX
PALMA Vecchio	XIIIb
PARMIGIANO	VI
PATENIER, Joachim	VIIId
PELLEGRINI, Giovanni Antonio	XIII
PERRONNEAU, Jean-Baptiste	XIX
PERUGINO, Pietro	IV
PESELLINO	III
PIERO di Cosimo	IV, VI
PIERO della Francesca	III
PINTORICCHIO	IV
PISANELLO	VIIIb
PISSARRO, Camille	XXI, XXII
PITTONI, Giovanni Battista	XIII
POEL, Egbert van der	X

Artist	*Room No.*
POLLAIUOLO, Antonio and Piero del	IV, VIII
PONTORMO	VI
PORDENONE	XIIIb
POTTER, Paulus	X
POUSSIN, Nicolas	XVIIb, XX
PREDA, Giovanni Ambrogio	XIIIa
PROVOOST, Jan	VIIId

R

RAPHAEL	VI
REMBRANDT van Rijn	XI
RENI, Guido	XVIIa, XVIIc
RENOIR, Pierre-Auguste	XXI, XXII
REYNOLDS, Sir Joshua	XVI
RIBERA, Jusepe de	XVIIa
RICCI, Sebastiano	XIII
ROBERTI, Ercole de'	VIIIa
ROMANINO, Girolamo	XVIId
ROSA, Salvator	XVIIb, XVIIc
RUBENS, Peter Paul	XIV
RUISDAEL, Jacob van	X, XII
RUYSDAEL, Salomon van	X

S

SAENREDAM, Pieter	X, XII
SARTO, Andrea del	VI
SASSETTA	II

Artist	Room No.
SASSOFERRATO	XVIIa, XVIIc
SAVOLDO, Giovanni Girolamo	XVIId
SCHALCKEN, Godfried	X
SEBASTIANO del Piombo	VI, VII
SEGNA di Bonaventura	I
SEURAT, Georges	XXI
SIBERECHTS, Jan	XIV
SIGNORELLI, Luca	IV
SISLEY, Alfred	XXII
SOLARI, Andrea	XIIIa
SPINELLO Aretino	II
STEEN, Jan	X
STROZZI, Bernardo	XVIIc

T

TENIERS, David, the younger	XIV
TIEPOLO, Giambattista	XIII
TIEPOLO, Domenico	XIII
TINTORETTO	VII
TITIAN	VII
TOULOUSE-LAUTREC, Henri de	XXI
TRECK, Jan	X
TURA, Cosimo	VIIIa
TURNER, Joseph Mallord William	XV, XVI

U

UCCELLO, Paolo	III
UGOLINO di Nerio	I

Artist	Room No.

V

VALENTIN, Le	XVIIa
VELAZQUEZ, Diego	XVIII
VELDE, Adriaen van de	X
VELDE, Esaias van de	X
VELDE, Willem van de, the younger	X, XII
VELSEN, Jacob van	X
VERMEER, Johannes	XII
VERONESE, Paolo	VII
VERROCCHIO, Andrea del	VIIIc
VIVARINI, Antonio	I
VLIEGER, Simon de	X
VRIES, Roelof van	X
VROOM, Cornelis	X

W

WALSCAPPELLE, Jacob van	X
WATTEAU, Antoine	XIX
WERFF, Adriaen van der	X
WEYDEN, Rogier van der	VIIId
WILSON, Richard	XVI
WILTON DIPTYCH	II
WITTE, Emanuel de	X
WOUWERMANS, Philips	X, XII
WIJNANTS, Jan	X, XII
WTEWAEL, Joachim	X

Artist   *Room No.*

Z

ZAIS, Giuseppe   XIII
ZOPPO, Marco   VIIIa
ZURBARÁN, Francisco de   XVIII

INFORMATION

The Gallery is open

Weekdays: 10 a.m. until 6 p.m.

Sundays: 2 p.m. until 6 p.m.

Note. In recent years it has been possible for the Gallery to remain open until 9 p.m. on Tuesdays and Thursdays during the summer months.

Closed Christmas Eve, Christmas Day and Good Friday.

The Information and Photographic Stall is on the West side of the Main Entrance. The Main Publications Stall is on the East side of the Main Entrance. Open:—

Monday-Friday: 10 a.m. until 5.40 p.m.

Saturday: 10 a.m. until 5 p.m.

Sunday: 3 p.m. until 5.30 p.m.

The Restaurant is on the Ground Floor and is approached from the East side of the Main Entrance. Open:—

Weekdays: 10 a.m. until 3 p.m.
3.30 p.m. until 5.15 p.m.

Sundays: 2 p.m. until 5 p.m.